UWM
BOOKS-

229-4201

FA 1800 338-4550

P9-CAN-512

The At-Risk Student

Evelyn Hunt Ogden, Ed.D.
Vito Germinario, Ed.D.

The at-risk student

ANSWERS FOR EDUCATORS

TECHNOMIC
PUBLISHING CO., INC.

LANCASTER · BASEL

Published in the Western Hemisphere by
Technomic Publishing Company, Inc.
851 New Holland Avenue
Box 3535
Lancaster, Pennsylvania 17604 U.S.A.

Distributed in the Rest of the World by
Technomic Publishing AG

©1988 by Technomic Publishing Company, Inc.
All rights reserved

No part of this publication may be reproduced, stored in a
retrieval system, or transmitted, in any form or by any means,
electronic, mechanical, photocopying, recording, or otherwise,
without the prior written permission of the publisher.

Printed in the United States of America
10 9 8 7 6 5 4

Main entry under title:
    The At-Risk Student: Answers for Educators

A Technomic Publishing Company book
Bibliography: p. 165
Includes index p. 169

Library of Congress Card No. 87-51632
ISBN No. 87762-573-5

29.95

To the following individuals who made a difference to students and in the profession to education:

Ruth Mancuso

Former president and member of the New Jersey Board of Education, she always applied her high standards, intelligence, and dedication to promote excellence in education during many years of service.

Mary Cudemo Schurig

A personal and professional inspiration, she has shown throughout her long career that commitment to student assistance does have an effect.

Robert W. Ward

The late director of program development, New Jersey Department of Education, he provided vision, leadership, and unswerving commitment, in the state and nationally, to the development of educational programs that truly work.

Table of Contents

Foreword

Sometimes one has to explain *why* a book has been written. This one requires no such justification. Consider these figures derived from news articles and editorials in the nation's press:

— Student suicide has increased 140 percent.
— Teenage homicide increased 232 percent.
— Juvenile delinquency rates rose by 131 percent.
— The illegitimate birth rate increased by 141 percent.

Add to this array of statistics over five hundred pieces of legislation introduced in the states concerning AIDS (acquired immune deficiency syndrome), many of which call for an educational component.

Few schools in the land have not been touched by any of these problems. When alcohol and drugs are added, the daily dilemmas of coping with these chemicals cast large shadows in the lives of parents, teachers and school administrators.

Recently at a national conference in Denver, Colorado, attended by more than six hundred school administrators, state legislators, teachers, governors and higher education officials, calls were repeatedly made for dealing with *at-risk students*. Some attendees concluded that a failure to respond to this *most compelling agenda* would threaten America's position as a world economic power.

Evelyn Ogden and Vito Germinario are front-line public school educators. Their experience collectively includes the school principalship, state education department leadership, classroom teaching and currently central office administration. They have directly dealt with the problems about which they have written.

Thus, this is not an "armchair" treatment of problems in the abstract. It is for all citizens and educators who must confront the sobering reality of life in the late twentieth century with students in schools.

Gone are the days when the most controversial problem might be a complaint about *Catcher in the Rye*, or smoking in the boy's room during passing periods. Student suicide and homicide have replaced these problems and make them appear tame indeed by comparison.

Drs. Ogden and Germinario have approached these problems from the perspective that while the schools must deal with them, they must remain firmly committed to their *educational mission* as a first priority. That theme is what anchors their vision and this book.

The challenge of the *at-risk student* is one we cannot afford to refuse. In some measure the response of today's citizens and educators will be felt by everyone in the years ahead.

FENWICK W. ENGLISH
Professor and Chair
Department of Educational Administration
College of Education
University of Cincinnati
Series Editor

Acknowledgements

Of the many people to whom we are indebted for writing this book, we would like to give special recognition to:

Fenwick English, Professor and Chair, Department of Educational Administration, University of Cincinnati, who identified a need for this book, guided the development of the content and served as editor.

Betty Steffy, Superintendent, Moorestown Township Public Schools, who encouraged us throughout this endeavor, and showed by her example that problems that put students at risk can be effectively managed.

Members of the Student Assistance Teams, in Moorestown Township Public Schools, who participated in the development and implementation of programs to assist students at risk.

Sandra Morgan, Program Coordinator, Drug and Alcohol Section, Pennsylvania Department of Education, who shared with us her expertise and long experience in the development of proactive student assistance programs.

Diana Robinson, a psychiatric nurse who contributed to the chapter on eating disorders and who assisted in editing the drafts.

Janet Jessel and Elizabeth Casey, who spent many hours editing the drafts and making recommendations to improve the work.

Mary Spillane, who typed the manuscript, made the corrections and remained as always cheerful, positive and highly efficient.

To all of them our warmest thanks!

Introduction

All children are at times students-at-risk and there is a portion of every school population that consistently shows a lack of the necessary intellectual, emotional and/or social skills to take full advantage of the educational opportunities available to them. Often these students become disenchanted, and ultimately openly or passively reject school—they are then students-at-high-risk.

The purpose of the school is to maximize learning for all students. The most obvious way in which schools attempt to carry out their mission is through direct instruction in the curriculum areas. However, another way of maximizing learning is by controlling or eliminating the effects of those factors which limit the learning and potential of children.

There are several reasons why teachers and administrators should be increasingly concerned with understanding and managing the factors that place limits on learning.

The first reason for concern is the question of equity in access to education. As laws and policies have been implemented to educate the disabled child, the bilingual child, the gifted child, etc., so it can be argued that the disaffected students, the majority of whom have normal intelligence, require specialized programs to truly benefit from their educational experience.

The second is that a variety of social problems are, at least in part, the result of an inadequate education. Equity issues aside, it is argued that our society can avoid more costly problems in the future by investing in the development of all its youth. A poorly educated person is more likely to require social welfare and institutional services and is increasingly more likely to be involved in the legal system as a result of criminal activities. In these very human terms, the cost of poor schooling may be significantly higher than the costs associated with good schooling.

A third reason is that there are changing societal expectations of schools in dealing with issues that were traditionally addressed within the family. The parents of at least 40 percent of the children born this year will divorce. One in four girls will become pregnant at least once during her high school years. Only one in one thousand college freshmen women plans a career as a homemaker.

Increasingly, parents will look to schools for help. Their first concern will be provision for a secure environment for their children as parents continue to pursue their own family needs and interests. But, more importantly, schools will be asked to assume a direct role in the teaching of essential life skills that were traditionally within the domain of family and church.

Fourth, disaffected or at-risk students have potentially negative effects on the attitude, behavior and achievement of other students.

It is our hope that this book will assist teachers, principals, and central administrators to develop school programs and classroom strategies to help educate the at-risk learners. Specifically, this book will address a wide variety of philosophical, sociological and instructional phenomena that will help establish a climate for identifying and assisting high-risk students.

It should be noted that this publication will deal only with those skills and activities that are within the normal reach of teachers and administrators. Thus, concepts related to effective schools and effective teacher research (Brookover and Lezotte, 1976; Ogden et al., 1982) will be used as a basic framework from which any strategies or programs should evolve.

Although many prevention and intervention techniques are discussed in this book, we believe that the role of the school staff is not to become therapists! Most of the problems or learning distractors discussed in this book can be addressed by the day-to-day actions of the school staff in their interaction with students in the classroom. In such cases as drug addiction, attempted suicide, child abuse, or other major dysfunctional behavior, the role of the school should be to identify and refer the child to trained outside experts.

To facilitate ease of use, the book is organized into sections reflecting prevention and intervention strategies at various grade intervals. These strategies include establishing and enforcing expectations, direct instruction to reduce risk, student assistance and direct intervention. Additionally, the book deals with the role central office administrators and school boards must play in the development and support of programs to maximize learning for high-risk students.

Essentially, the topics addressed in grades K–4 emphasize PREVENTION strategies directly related to what the principal and classroom teachers can do to promote a school and classroom climate that facilitates the teaching of specific life skills. Further, a model for group problem solving and crisis intervention is presented.

The middle grade program discussed in the book deals primarily with early INTERVENTION strategies which help remediate individual student life skill deficiencies that serve to limit a student's academic growth and social adjustment.

Strategies directed at serving high school populations deal with DIRECT INTERVENTION mechanisms where school personnel actively involve parents in obtaining professional assistance for their child who, at this point, may be experiencing emotional distress or chemical dependency.

It is important to understand that programs aimed at assuring student wellness need to be carefully articulated throughout a child's educational experience. A comprehensive plan makes it possible for schools to take advantage of the accumulated learnings, attitudes, and behaviors developed by the child in previous grades. Further, it provides a stable environment to promote specific teaching behaviors aimed at maintaining a positive class climate and the teaching and reinforcement of needed life skills. Just as a good curriculum is aligned to ensure sequential presentation of content, so a conscientious program to enrich the learning environment must be designed to service students in a systematic, consistent manner throughout their school experience.

This book is guided by several basic premises that will provide focus to those educators who are committed to educating at-risk students. Administrators and teachers can:

— identify situations which are risks to learning and opportunities to enhance learning
— implement programs which will maximize the climate for learning
— prepare for the periodic crises facing children in their schools and classrooms and minimize the negative effects of such problems
— teach students behaviors and skills which promote further learning and reduce the chances of involvement in destructive behavior
— improve student achievement by more systematically applying what is known about educating children

This book is designed to serve as a guide to promoting student well-being and learning. Further, the organization of the book provides a practical framework by which specific high-risk student behaviors can be addressed. Finally, this book can serve as a desk reference that provides specific guidelines, procedures and correspondence needed to plan effectively a total student assistance program or to respond to the variety of crisis situations confronting today's schools.

EVELYN HUNT OGDEN
East Brunswick

VITO GERMINARIO
Moorestown

CHAPTER 1

Promoting Achievement and Developing School Wellness

The purpose of the school is to promote pupil learning. To achieve this purpose the school must have and deliver a well-defined and appropriate curriculum. In addition, the school must strive to develop an environment which maximizes learning and minimizes conditions which interfere with learning. The degree to which a school accomplishes these objectives is the measure of its degree of "wellness."

A "well" student is defined as one who is achieving at a rate commensurate with his or her ability, has a positive attitude toward self, teachers and school, has positive relationships with peers and does not exhibit destructive behaviors. A "well" school is one which has assessed the learning environment of the school and has taken action to reduce or eliminate impediments to learning. It is a school, therefore, in which students of all types are achieving academically. This means there is a positive attitude toward school and staff, high expectations, and freedom from destructive behaviors in the school environment. Since school is only part of a student's or a teacher's or an administrator's life, the school does not control all the variables which affect wellness. Therefore, schools cannot be totally well, and individual students cannot be totally well in terms of learning at all times. However, principals, teachers, counselors, and support staff can have profound effects on the degree of wellness of the school and students individually. It is a matter of choice within a continuum.

THE ROLE OF THE SCHOOL

The role of the administrators and teachers includes:
— assessing the school climate and the individual needs of students

1

- setting expectations for improvement
- planning for the reduction or elimination of learning distractors
- planning activities and approaches for enhancing the learning environment
- planning for crises
- implementing, intervention monitoring and evaluating

It is not the role of the school staff to become therapists. The problems or learning distractors discussed in this book can be addressed by the day-to-day action of the staff in their interaction with students in the classroom. In cases such as drug addiction, attempted suicide, child abuse, or major dysfunctional behavior the role of the school should be to identify and refer the child to trained outside experts. During or following treatment the school regains a role in providing support for the student in the school environment.

THE RATIONALE FOR A K–12 APPROACH

High and consistent expectations are essential if students are to achieve throughout their school experience and be prepared to function effectively as adults. For the student in school the route is continuous in time, from kindergarten to graduation. The student brings to the next grade or next school the accumulated learning, attitudes and behaviors developed in previous grades or schools. It makes sense, then, that just as sound curriculum is articulated from K throughout 12, the design and development of the learning environment be similarly articulated from K through 12. However, if this is not possible the school or even the classroom can be the focus of an effective plan.

COMPONENTS OF A COMPREHENSIVE PROGRAM

There are several components of a comprehensive program to promote learning:
- Assessment–Determining the needs and opportunities is the first step in developing a program to promote learning and to reduce risk. The assessment should be done on three levels: the school, the classroom and the individual student.
- Expectations–Expectations are the norms and guidelines for developing activities as well as the criteria by which success

or failure is measured. Expectations take many forms in schools. The most formal expectations are those set by the school board as policies. Within the society of the school they have the force of law. Discipline codes, operating procedures, and instructional objectives are all examples of expectations.

— Student Assistance—Student assistance includes all the planned and spontaneous ways schools react to aiding students to cope with new situations, problems and learning opportunities. Student assistance activities include formal programs such as those provided by the guidance department, and the informal but important extra support given to a child by his teacher during a time of crisis.

— Curriculum—Curriculum in a comprehensive program to enhance the learning environment refers to instruction designed primarily: to increase the student's ability to learn how to learn, to increase the student's ability to resist involvement in destructive activities, and to promote positive involvement with school peers and society.

— Communications—Communicating is an important part of any program development effort. Staff, students, parents and the community have to be aware of the need for a program, the expectations, the procedures and activities to be implemented and how the program will be evaluated. Procedures for gaining input from affected groups and the communication of developing plans should be one of the first components addressed in program development.

— Training—As the parts of the program are ready for implementation, training in some form is necessary. The training for some components can be simple and covered in a faculty meeting. More complex components may require a series of training sessions.

— Monitoring—Very few programs fail because of their design or the effectiveness of the proposed strategies. Most programs which fail, fail because they were never really implemented as designed. Once the plan for new procedures or a comprehensive program has been accepted, training has taken place, and the program initiated, then systematic monitoring of implementation must begin.

— Evaluation—Once the program has been implemented and monitoring indicates that activities are being conducted according to the plan, it is time to evaluate the program to determine if the expectations/objectives are being met.

The foundation of a student wellness program has its roots in the structure and climate of the school culture. To date, much has been written about the nature of effective schools and classrooms. It is essential that this information is carefully studied and that school professionals assess their practices in relation to this emerging body of research.

SCHOOLS THAT MAXIMIZE LEARNING

A great deal is known about the general characteristics of effective schools. A systematic effort to apply the concepts related to this increasing body of research can have a positive effect on school climate and student achievement. Specifically, effective schools studies have identified several factors that most often contribute to higher levels of student performance (Brookover and Lezotte, 1976; Ogden, et al., 1982). Most often, the characteristics include:

- an orderly learning environment with minimum classroom disruption
- an emphasis on maximizing instructional use of time
- an academic emphasis
- an aligned curriculum matched to specific objectives and assessment procedures
- a clear communication of high expectations for all learners
- an ongoing monitoring of achievement by the principal and teachers
- a clear indication that the principal is functioning as the school's instructional leader

Although schools cannot directly counter the negatives to which children are exposed, effective planning for the improvement of the learning climate can produce significant achievement and behavioral gains.

Thus, any program to help ensure student well-being must first take the necessary steps to plan a school and ultimately a classroom environment that maximizes the potential for learning. This phenomenon is important since a strong relationship exists between poor academic achievement in early grades, increased student dissatisfaction with school, disengagement within the classroom, increased high school dropout rates, and a variety of high-risk behaviors.

CLASSROOMS THAT MAXIMIZE LEARNING

Current teacher effectiveness research forms the basis from which an assessment can be made regarding the effects of teacher behavior upon a variety of measurable student outcomes. This is not to suggest that there is a single most effective model for teaching. Instead, this research attempts to isolate specific behaviors and routines that a teacher can consciously use to improve classroom processes. Knowledge and application of concepts related to this body of research will more effectively allow teachers to match the content taught and methodology used with the uniqueness of his/her students. Essentially, knowledge and application of these principles will improve the quality of teacher decisions regarding the impact of these behaviors on student learning.

Class Climate

It is not unusual for students and their parents to identify classrooms where a positive feeling tone exists. These feelings usually are observed in classrooms where a warm, supportive environment is in effect. Further, these classrooms tend to promote an atmosphere where children feel comfortable to raise their hands, to take an active part in the learning process, to take more chances, and where tolerance is exhibited for student mistakes.

Recent studies have begun to identify specific climate factors that are linked in both correlation and experimental studies to student gains.

The following discussion will attempt to summarize some of the major contributions of this research.

Students are likely to work better and achieve at higher levels in an atmosphere that assumes that they can and will succeed in the tasks established by the teacher. There is a clear relationship between achievement gains in average and below average ability level students and the number of successful responses they give in a classroom. Thus, teachers must plan situations and events that are designed specifically to provide opportunities for these students to get right answers and thus earn the praise and reinforcement associated with high achievement (Brophy, 1981).

As rudimentary as this may sound, consistent evidence exists

(Good, 1982) to support the contention that typical classrooms do not provide equal opportunity for student involvement and success. Most teachers tend to call on those students that can be consistently depended upon to provide a correct answer. This is primarily done so that: (1) a student not expected to know the answer does not get embarrassed, (2) to ensure that the students in the class hear a correct and thoughtful reply, and (3) to provide a certain degree of teacher reward associated with high quality student performances (Kerman, 1980). This phenomenon produces an interesting paradox. Students will soon realize that they are less likely to be called on; consequently, because they are not actually engaged in classroom interaction they become less able. Knowing that they probably will not be called upon, many students are likely to seek attention and success through dysfunctional means or unresponsively drift through school.

Taking time to listen to a student who wishes to contribute to the class or offer a personal experience clearly establishes a climate where a student feels he/she is important. A variety of studies link this notion of personal regard (Kerman, 1980) to a student's willingness to engage in learning and, thus increase the likelihood of achievement.

All too often, the majority of feedback students receive in a classroom is short praise or correction. The ongoing stream of one-liners such as "good," "okay," "no," "wrong," etc., add little to a student's feeling of well-being in the classroom. Feedback has proved to be a powerful tool in motivating students and ensuring the correctness of original learning (Hunter, 1986). Praise can and should be used to extend pupil–teacher contact and to encourage and reinforce desired behaviors. Yet, there is significant evidence to support the idea that less able students actually receive less praise than higher achieving students (Good, Biddle, Brophy, 1975). This was true even when less able students provided correct answers.

This pattern of inequality for personal regard was evidenced in the teacher's willingness to accept student feelings (Adams and Biddle, 1970); listen to students (Rest, 1979); accepting feelings (Brophy and Good, 1984); and showing personal interest (Perkins, 1965).

Hunter (1985) has provided a vehicle to help ensure that students receive appropriate and intended feedback to their responses. She suggests that each student comment/response should be "dignified" so that the student feels he/she has made an important contribution to the class. Secondly, the teachers should "probe" for the correct answer so that the students in the class will receive appropriate information. Finally, regardless of correctness of student response, he/she should be held "accountable" for providing information relative to the topic at a future time during the lesson. Thus, an incorrect student response should be followed by a clarifying statement emphasizing the correct and/or thoughtful parts of a student's comments; then, through a series of direct questions, the teacher should help "draw out" the correct response; and finally, regardless of the success achieved by the student, he/she is given credit for his/her contributions and told that he/she will be again asked to share his/her thoughts at a later time in the lesson.

Along the same line, Rosenshine and Furst (1971) indicate five ways of using student ideas during interaction:

1. Acknowledging a student's response by literally repeating the answer out loud to the rest of the class
2. Modifying the student's response by putting it into different words so that it is more understandable or more appropriate but still conveys the idea originated by the student
3. Applying the student's response to some situation; using it as an explanation for some event or occurrence
4. Comparing the student's response to something in the text, something already discussed, some concurrent similar event
5. Summarizing the responses made by students and using them to draw a conclusion or make a point.

Clear Expectations/Quality Use of Time

Classrooms characterized by positive class climates and high levels of achievement show good organizational structure and a high proportion of time spent in instructional activities. While school schedules throughout the country vary little in terms of the time allocated for learning, differences as great as nine hours a week have been found among schools in the amount of time spent on instruction (Goodlad, 1984).

Teachers need to teach routines and clearly establish expectations during the first few weeks of school. A study of teachers in eleven junior high schools found that more effective teachers were more likely to give students copies of rules, homework procedures, etc. (Everston, 1980). Other such "Standard Operating Procedures" for students have been formalized and distributed to students to help establish clear expectations, provide avenues for classroom success, and actively engage parents in assuring that students meet their responsibilities.

Additionally, classroom practices such as giving clear directions, managing transitional times, providing several different learning activities throughout the lesson, monitoring student performance, providing corrective feedback, and maintaining a positive management style all are closely linked to the effective use of class time.

Direct Instruction

Taking the necessary steps to maintain a high degree of instructional time does not necessarily ensure increased levels of student achievement. Specific strategies typically associated with direct instructional models are correlated to greater achievement, particularly in basic skill development (Rosenshine, 1979; Cummings, 1980). The model essentially begins with a diagnosis of students to determine their prerequisite skills for certain learning tasks. Subsequent instructions are broken down into small incremental steps or clusters from which learning gains have been reported (Brophy, 1981).

A preinstructional set is then established which typically includes a clear statement of objective and expectation, a description of materials and procedures to be used, and an explanation of the significance of the task so that the lesson becomes more meaningful to students. Further, establishing this mental set is used to:

— build interest and develop willingness
— provide advance organization on a common frame of reference for the lesson to follow
— relate clearly what is to follow
— provide a logical "jumping off" point for the lesson (Bruce, 1976)

The teacher must then provide specific instruction directed toward the achievement of lesson objectives. This active instruction from the teacher has proven to show measurable learning dividends (Brophy and Good, 1985). Such active instruction should include mechanisms actively to involve students in learning, provisions for the ongoing monitoring of student understanding, demonstrations and other opportunities for learning through observation and imitation (modeling), and allowances of sufficient time for students to practice a new skill under the direct supervision of the teacher. During this time, the teacher walks among the students providing support, encouragement, praise, individual assistance, etc. Through this monitoring of student performance, a teacher is given an opportunity to use a number of behaviors that have proven to be directly related to achievement.

Frequent reactions to student misbehavior are counterproductive to learning. Belittling, ridiculing, excessive scolding and shouting and criticizing are related to low achievement (Turkinoff, et al., 1975). Effective teachers have the ability to minimize potential problems by anticipating them and planning student activities that effectively use class time.

Proactive Management Style

Minor student disturbances are inevitable. Each time a student misbehaves, the teacher has a variety of options to effectively stop the misbehavior. Essentially, the teacher must choose that option which will detract as little as possible from instruction and the learning environment. Cummings (1983) supports the use of the "Law of Least Intervention" which aids teachers in choosing the most unobtrusive disciplinary response to minor misbehavior so that distraction from instruction is minimized. Using a sequential set of teacher responses to student misbehavior, it is suggested that reactive management behaviors (shouting, criticizing, etc.) will be reduced while characteristics of pleasant class climate can be maintained. (For complete list of minimal intervention strategies, see Cummings, *Managing to Teach*, 1983.)

Learning Style

Every student has a preferred learning style. While most students can learn through a variety of sensory stimuli and within different learning environments, enough research is available to support the notion of teaching through learning styles to improve student learning (Dunn and Dunn, et al.).

Learning style is comprised of a combination of environmental, emotional, sociological, physical, and psychological elements that permit individuals to receive, store, and use knowledge or abilities (Dunn and Dunn, 1983). Information concerning the effectiveness of teaching students through individual learning styles is now available through a wide network of well-conceived research studies at all grade levels. Although it is not the authors' intent to promote the use of the teaching through learning styles as an efficient methodology for all learners, enough verifiable evidence exists from both an empirical and common sense orientation to support the concept as a viable means to improve student achievement. This concept can be especially significant for those students whose learning style is so idiosyncratic that attempts to educate through traditional methods have been unsuccessful.

MAXIMIZING LEARNING
CLASSROOM WELLNESS INVENTORY

Following is a list of descriptive statements which are associated with the promotion of learning in the classroom. Indicate the degree to which you think your classroom matches the description. There is no passing score. Areas in which you rate your classroom below 5 are areas in which improvement can be expected to result in increased learning.

		Low				High
1.	The following groups of students have absentee rates of less than 5%:					
	a. High Achieving	1	2	3	4	5
	b. Average	1	2	3	4	5
	c. Low Achieving	1	2	3	4	5
2.	I am absent less than 3.5% of the time.	1	2	3	4	5
3.	I maximize classroom instruction time by:					
	a. Having clear standard procedures for classroom management	1	2	3	4	5
	b. Having materials and activities organized in advance	1	2	3	4	5
4.	Students in my class do not interrupt when I am speaking.	1	2	3	4	5
5.	Students in my class respect each other when they are asking or answering a question.	1	2	3	4	5
6.	Students are accepting of differences among their fellow students.	1	2	3	4	5
7.	I am aware when a student is having a personal problem and communicate my understanding.	1	2	3	4	5
8.	I do not think of the children who learn at a slower rate as a burden.	1	2	3	4	5
9.	I encourage gifted students to take intellectual risks and use higher level thinking skills.	1	2	3	4	5
10.	Students in my class feel successful.	1	2	3	4	5
11.	Each lesson I teach includes:					
	a. An objective communicated to the class	1	2	3	4	5
	b. Direct instruction of content	1	2	3	4	5
	c. Assessment of what was learned	1	2	3	4	5
	d. Summary activity	1	2	3	4	5
12.	Students work with other students of varying ability and in whole group activities.	1	2	3	4	5
13.	Students are not labeled by other students, by me, or by the way I organize the class.	1	2	3	4	5
14.	All types of students respond to an equal number of questions.	1	2	3	4	5
15.	I wait as long for answers from students of lesser ability as I do for those of high ability.	1	2	3	4	5
16.	I assess the achievement of my students frequently and modify my instruction to meet needs.	1	2	3	4	5
17.	Students achieve the objectives of the curriculum and are ready for the next level class.	1	2	3	4	5
18.	I communicate with parents in a manner which has them support what is happening in class.	1	2	3	4	5

Maintenance of Enthusiasm Toward Task

There is an increasing amount of evidence to support the significant role a teacher serves in fostering student achievement and well-being. Teachers do make a difference. Similarly, specific teaching behaviors make a difference. Through an endless stream of verbal and non-verbal, intended and unintended messages, teachers play a pivotal role in the intellectual, social and emotional well-being of students. Thus, it becomes essential that all educators continue to look upon the research embodied in the science of teaching as a guide to school and classroom practices. Moreover, they must go about their task with a high degree of commitment and enthusiasm. It is through the genuineness of effort that students in our schools grow to their fullest potential.

The "Wellness Inventory," shown at left, will serve as a self-evaluation for teachers to assess the overall learning climate in their classes. Consistently high scores help ensure adherence to the concepts related to the positive student outcomes previously discussed. This inventory is not intended to provide categorical evidence as to the degree of wellness in a class. Thus, an overall optimum "wellness score" is not provided. Instead, each item should be studied separately with the assumption that improving a particular classroom phenomenon will ultimately improve the overall nature of classroom climate and student learning.

SUMMARY

The purpose of this chapter was to emphasize the importance of academic achievement as an essential prerequisite to student well-being. Further, it provided a brief analysis of teacher behaviors and procedures that are closely linked to the maintenance of a positive class climate and increased levels of student achievement.

It is upon the basic premises established above that the instructional and programmatic considerations for any attempt at educating all students, and most importantly high-risk students, should be founded.

CHAPTER 2

Managing Risks to
Maximize Learning: Grades K–4

Most children like school and this is especially true for those in early grades. However, there is considerable evidence to suggest that dysfunctional student behaviors, which influence a child's achievement levels and attitudes toward school, can be identified as early as kindergarten. One need only review student records to understand the uncanny accuracy of primary teachers in identifying those students who do, in fact, experience difficulty in taking full advantage of the educational opportunities made available to them in later years.

In extreme cases, such students can become school phobic, thus, actively resisting the formal efforts of school personnel. In other cases, the symptoms are mild, yet significant enough to interfere with ability to maximize learning potential. Lack of success in school can be a major contributor to dysfunctional behavior. Yet, poor health, perceived attitudes of teachers, unstable peer relations, and the dynamics of the home can all add to high-risk behaviors.

The trials and tribulations of all young children during the formative school years, as they try to formulate their piece of the world, are difficult. All children experience risks which can limit learning. Most young people make it, and as a result of their experiences emerge as the person they are satisfied to be and meet with the approval and pride from family and friends.

Students who achieve in school and feel successful as a result of that achievement have positive attitudes toward school and themselves. Teachers, principals, and parents have major responsibilities in establishing a climate for learning. Learning in the school goes beyond the content areas, such as reading and math and includes learning to live effectively in society. A significant portion of the young child's "society" is the school. What the teachers and principal do enhances or limits the child's ability to function in that society, to build a base for future interactions in society and to succeed as a learner.

In addition to the direct effect on individual children of the learning climate, there are significant effects of such instruction on the total school society of children, teachers, administrators and parents. Teachers in orderly task oriented schools experience less stress; students are not intimidated by the actions of other students; and principals have time to focus on instruction rather than discipline.

This chapter will present a variety of school programs and instructional strategies aimed at proactively developing the learning environment of all students. Models for shaping school norms, curriculum planning, group problem solving and crisis intervention will be developed.

ESTABLISHING AND REINFORCING POSITIVE NORMS

The literature on effective schools consistently stresses the need for high expectations in schools (Rosenthal, 1968; Brookover, 1977; Ogden, et al., 1980). Teachers and principals in successful schools believe students (all students) can learn. In some ways it is a paradoxical situation. Does the staff believe the students can learn and therefore, they do learn? Or do the students learn and therefore, the staff believes they can learn? It is probably more of the former, staff positive beliefs come first. However, success takes more than a belief that students can learn; it takes a commitment that all students "will" learn. Expectations always exist in schools whether they are implied or formally stated. In order to have a maximum impact on learning, expectations need to be agreed upon by staff, stated in understandable terms, and used as the base for learning and the interactions of the society within the school.

Expectations for Students

One way of communicating expectations is to create a student job description. This can be done by an individual teacher or by a committee. The job description lists in simple terms what is expected from the student.

This job description must be communicated to students and their parents. Appropriate opportunity should be given for the discussion of its content so that a clear understanding of role and expectations is established. Exact items included in a job description should, to a large degree, represent the unique needs of the teacher

```
┌─────────────────────────────────────────────────────────────────────┐
│                      Student Job Description                          │
│                                                                       │
│   I get enough sleep.                                                 │
│   I eat a nutritious breakfast.              GRADES K–3               │
│   I come to school on time.                                          │
│   I come to school ready to learn.                                   │
│   I come to school with all my supplies.                            │
│   I follow all classroom rules.                                     │
│   I am courteous to my teachers.                                    │
│   I am considerate of my classmates.                                │
│   I do my best to complete all my classwork.                        │
│   I have a special study place at home.                             │
│   I have a special time every day when I do my school work at home. │
│   I complete my homework and return it to school when done.         │
│   I talk to my parents about my homework.                           │
│   I talk to my parents about any problems I may be having in school.│
└─────────────────────────────────────────────────────────────────────┘
```

and his/her students. Yet, a core of minimum expectancies should be consistently administered and communicated throughout the school. It is advisable that the school produce a simple handbook describing how these core expectations affect students at each grade level within the school.

Classroom Expectations

Expectations also need to be set and communicated for each class. "Today we are going to learn -----." Students need to know if they are meeting teacher expectations. However, praise should be handed out with honest care. It loses its impact when dispensed after every student response. In general, praise has a more positive effect on low-achieving students than high-achieving students (Brophy, 1980).

In addition to communicating positive expectations, classroom climate can be negatively affected by indirect communication of low expectation. Studies have shown that teachers call more often on the higher-achieving students and are more patient in waiting for their response (Brophy, 1980). Other students in the class are quick to pick up on these clues.

Informal school norms may also place limits on learning. When teachers talk about students and their classes they frequently show low expectations for certain students. "Johnny is really slowing down the class; however, what can you expect with his 'home life'?" In a school with an expected norm that children "will learn" such questions are met with, "What are you doing in class to work with Johnny?"

Clearly, it is the role of the school principal to monitor the school climate so that positive expectations and a feeling that all students can learn is maintained. Failure to effectively monitor the impact of expectations will, without doubt, cause negative sentiments to spiral. Thus, feelings concerning students' inability to learn will become self-fulfilled, ultimately causing a negative impact on organizational climate and student well-being.

Shaping School Norms

While the individual teacher controls the climate within the class, the principal has the major responsibility of establishing school guides and norms. Expectations concerning student behavior should be established for playground, cafeteria, halls, assemblies as well as toward visitors. While students come from different cultural backgrounds and what constitutes good manners may have some differences, the school is a society which must establish its own norms for behavior.

Sets of expected behaviors should be established by the staff and taught to students. Older students may participate in setting the expectations. For example, an assembly provides a good opportunity to teach children how to behave in a large group, how to show their appreciation of something they like, how to show respect even when they become bored. A set of written expectations and a discussion before and after the event can ease the way for a productive activity. Cafeterias are places where social expectations can and should be taught. Frequently, schools view cafeterias as places to be "controlled." Controlled cafeterias do reduce the chances of some students being victimized by other children. However, positive expectations, instruction and reinforcement can make the cafeteria a learning experience and a place where stress is reduced and positive behaviors fostered.

Standard Operating Procedures

Standard operating procedures are a specific means for achieving high expectations. Young children accept the authority of adults and look to them as models. However, they have to be taught what is expected of them in school. Good standard operating procedures in the classroom can maximize time for learning and reduce opportunities for negative behaviors. SOP's should be written, taught to students and reinforced from the first day of school. A typical SOP might include provisions such as the following:

– Sharpen pencils before class in the morning or before class after lunch.
– Keep three pencils in your desk.
– Line up for lunch one row at a time.
– In the morning put homework in the box on the counter.
– Put absentee notes in the box on the teacher's desk.
– When you want help during seat work, put the orange card on the top of your desk.

These procedures should be clearly communicated in both staff and parent/student handbooks. Further, specific expectations should be periodically reinforced by the teacher in the classroom, and by the principal through ongoing newsletters and parent meetings.

The principal and staff should also establish SOP's for the cafeteria, playground, assemblies, halls, and school buses.

Pupil Control

Even with high expectations and clear SOP's there will be a need for disciplinary steps. It has been well documented that in order to be effective, discipline must be simple, fair and consistent. Children need to know what the penalties are for certain actions, and that penalties will be applied equally and consistently to all students. To facilitate this process, each school should have a standard discipline code appropriate to the age of the children in the school. The code should set forth the list of infractions and list the consequences.

Parents and School Expectations

As previously indicated, parents should be well informed concerning the expectations, SOP's, and discipline code of the school. In some cases they can be involved in developing the procedures. In all cases, communicating with the parents is essential, so they can reinforce what the child is expected to do at school and at home.

Some schools have developed contracts with parents stating what the school and parents will each do to promote learning. Another

School Disciplinary Code

Specific situations may dictate adjustments in the disciplinary sequence.

Inappropriate Behavior	Consequence		
Misbehavior in the halls/lavatories *For example:* • running • noise/using profanity • pushing • fighting	1st offense Subsequent offenses	1. 2. 3. 4.	Conference and counseling with child, teacher/principal Parent contact/conference and counseling with student-principal/teacher After-school detention In-school suspension
Misbehavior on the playground *For example:* • fighting • throwing foreign objects • not responding to re-entry bell • pushing, talking in line • playing unapproved games • using profanity • disrespectful behavior toward aides	1st offense Subsequent offenses	1. 2. 3. 4. 5.	Conference and counseling with child-teacher/aide Conference with child-principal Parent contact/conference with principal/teacher and after-school detention Loss of playground privilege for designated period of time In-school suspension
Misbehavior in the cafeteria *For example:* • fighting, pushing • throwing food • running around tables • disrespectful behavior toward teacher/aides • using profanity	1st offense Subsequent offenses	1. 2. 3. 4.	Conference and counseling with child-teacher/aide Loss of playground privilege Parent contact/conference with child-principal/teacher Removal from cafeteria/Student will be sent home (with parent involvement) for the lunch period for a designated period of time and in-school suspension
Misbehavior in assemblies *For example:* • excessive talking during presentation • pushing or shoving while entering auditorium • booing and whistling during or after presentation	1st offense Subsequent offenses	1. 2. 3.	Conference and counseling with child-principal/teacher—with possible removal from assembly Parent contact-conference and counseling with child-principal/teacher Loss of assembly privilege

approach might be for the parent association and staff to develop a job description for parents. Such a job description might list specific things parents can do to assist the student complete his/her own job description. For example: set aside a time for homework, turn off the television when homework is being done. Development of a parent job description might be a project of the PTA.

Rewards

There should be recognized payoffs for students as they meet the expectations of the school. Not every behavior needs a specific reward; in fact, rewards as praise can become ineffective motivators. However, recognizing positive attitudes, behaviors and achievement are important to maintaining a learning climate. If one believes all children will learn and exhibits positive attitudes, then all children must have the opportunity to be rewarded. Some of the ways students might be rewarded are with:

— increased responsibility, e.g., taking information to the school office
— increased independence, e.g., deciding on what to do after completing an assignment

CURRICULUM TO REDUCE RISK, K–4

Schools can assist children to maximize learning by maintaining positive class climate, providing direct instruction and appropriately responding to specific situations. This section addresses the areas which are incorporated into the curriculum and delivered to all students through direct instruction and are designed to enhance learning in all areas of the school program.

Life Skills

No

There is increasing evidence to support the need for school curricula to address topics related to a wide variety of life skills (Roberts, et al., 1986). An analysis of behavioral patterns of adults in mental health clinics points toward the inadequate development of self-concepts and ill-developed communication, decision-making and/or social interaction skills as prime indicators of their inability to cope (Rutter, 1980). Not surprisingly, young children who are experiencing problems in school typically share these same shortcomings. Thus, the school must take an active role in teaching these needed life skills. It is assumed that satisfactory development of these skills will reduce the risk of atypical behavior in school. Further, the teaching of the appropriate information will reduce the possibility of drug abuse and other dysfunctional coping mechanisms a student might otherwise choose as he/she grows through his/her adolescent years.

Drugs and Mental Health

Sixty-one percent of high school seniors report that they have used drugs (United States Department of Education, 1986). The average grade for initial use of cigarettes is 5th, alcohol 6th, and marijuana 7th (Roberts, et al., 1986). The time to begin drug education is in kindergarten. The elementary curriculum should include:
— information on drugs and their effects
— development of decision-making and drug resistance skills
— coping skills
— development of positive peer relationships
— positive alternative to drugs

The content of the curriculum must take into account the age of the children. The kindergarten program would include, for example, a simple definition of "What is a drug." Learning that pills are not candy, that there are poisons in the home, and why we have rules. By 4th grade, the program would include the study of the effects of the two drugs they will encounter first, alcohol and nicotine. Developing skills in saying "no" to people who pressure them to try drugs must be emphasized.

Finally, social interaction skills must be taught to help students make and keep friends without using drugs as a vehicle for group acceptance. A good drug prevention curriculum, while aimed at preventing drug use, must also focus on developing positive self-image, developing friendships, coping with problems and developing decision-making skills that will ultimately contribute to maximizing learning throughout a student's school experience.

The drug prevention curriculum can be taught by a health teacher, nurse or the classroom teacher. It is important that the curriculum be coordinated throughout grades K–4 and that all children do in fact receive instruction. Specific activities can be altered to better meet the needs or interests of the students or the knowledge of the teacher. Yet, all objectives identified for a grade

"Here's Looking At You, 2000"*

Information Skills Bonding	K–1	2	3	4
Dangers of unknown substances	X	X		
Drugs and their effects	X	X	X	X
Definition of drugs	X	X	X	
Chemical dependency and the individual	X	X	X	
Chemical dependency in the family	X			X
Alcohol			X	X
Nicotine				X
Reasons why people use and don't use drugs			X	X
Risk factors and ways to reduce risks				X
Identification and evaluation of sources of information about drugs				X
Asking someone for something	X	X		
Abiding by ground rules for discussing sensitive topics in front of others	X	X	X	X
Making decisions	X			X
Asking someone to do something (assertiveness)		X		
Keeping out of trouble (self-control)			X	
Identifying sources of influence				X
Saying no to keep friends				X
Explaining that problems are normal	X	X		
Acknowledging feelings and dealing with them	X	X	X	
Helping others feel included	X	X	X	
Appreciating self as special	X	X	X	X
Identifying ways to take care of the body			X	X
Identifying healthy ways to have fun			X	X
Identifying personal strengths				X
Identifying others' strengths				X

*"Here's Looking At You, 2000." Roberts, Fitzmahan and Associates, Educational Services District #121, Seattle, Washington, 1986.

must be covered. As in all school programs effectiveness should be assessed annually. Finally, there should be definite plans for communicating with parents concerning the need, purpose and content of the program. This will help parents understand the importance of such a curriculum, and develop a support base for implementation.

The drug prevention curriculum can be developed locally if time, resources, and knowledge are available. Another approach is the adoption of a program which has evidence of being successful. The program "Here's Looking At You, 2000," developed by Roberts, Fitzmahan and Associates, the Educational Service District #121, in Seattle, Washington (revised 1986), is the type of program which should at least be reviewed before attempting to develop a new program (see scope and sequence below). The program is sequenced K–12 but the K–4 section can be used alone. It has been extensively field tested in schools throughout the country. It includes all the activities and materials needed for implementation of the program. It is sufficiently detailed that extensive training of teachers may not be needed. Importantly, the content is consistent with that recommended for the grade levels by the report of the United States Department of Education, *What Works: Schools Without Drugs* (1987).

Physical Education

For children in grades K–4 what happens on the playground has a profound effect on how he/she feels about school and how he/she relates to peers. The child who views him- or herself or is perceived by other children as unable to participate adequately in games is handicapped in the society of the child. What happens on the playground has impact in the classroom. Failure to develop sufficient physical skill to "hold one's own" with peers outside of school or in noninstructional play situations is a common cause for poor peer relations, failure to like school, and feelings of alienation. All these are negative characteristics associated with school failure, dropouts and risk of drug abuse.

In some elementary schools all of the physical education instruction is provided by the classroom teacher; in some schools a specialist provides at least part of the instruction. Elementary physical education should be developmental in nature. It should be approached in the same manner as any other subject. The achievement level of students should be assessed, specific objectives set and instruction designed to meet the objectives.

The physical fitness test of the President's Council on Physical Fitness, available through the American Association of Health, Physical Education and Recreation, is a good test which can be used to determine the needs and strengths of students.

The curriculum should be inclusive, not exclusive. In other words activities should not eliminate the least able, while giving the most able more practice. An example of such a practice is having students jump over a rope, where after each jump the rope is raised. When a student misses he is eliminated. Thus, the most skilled child in the class ends up with the most practice. If the rope is slanted all children can continue to jump and increase their level based on their ability (Mosston, 1966). No one would reduce the time a poor reader spent on developing reading skills; however, it happens too frequently in physical education classes. Physical activity should be designed to develop:

— agility
— strength
— balance
— flexibility

This developmental program can take place in the classroom between academic activities as well as during designated physical education class time.

The physical education teachers in the district, whether they provide the direct instruction to the elementary school children or not, should design a detailed curriculum for each grade. The curriculum should be based on the assessment results for that grade. Lists of remedial activities should be included for students with special needs.

The video recorder holds promise for helping the classroom teacher provide physical education. There are commercially available exercise programs which can be used in the class. In addition, where physical education staff is limited, the physical education staff can tape lessons which can be used by the classroom teacher.

If at all possible, remedial/adaptive physical education should be available and provided by a physical education teacher.

Cooperative Learning Programs

Typically, classroom goals and activities are structured around competitive tasks leading to individual achievement. Alone, these types of activities can promote a "win–lose" attitude and thus do little to promote school interaction, communication and other related cooperative skills. Studies associated with specific cooperative learning teaching strategies (see Johnson, Johnson, 1975) provide evidence to support the positive influence of noncompetitive learning ventures on psychological health, social competencies, motivation, self-esteem, positive attitudes toward school and achievement (Johnson, 1980).

Non-competitive types of activities are not designed simply to have children sit next to each other, share materials, or check each other's work. Instead, cooperative learning occurs when students have a responsibility for both individual learning within the group and for group product and process. Through this cooperative interaction, students receive group awards for completing group tasks, thus emphasizing the importance of the individual's responsibility not only to him-/herself, but also to the group.

It is through this positive goal interdependence among students that interactive skills such as cooperation and communication can be taught. As students learn these skills, they become better able to transfer them to other academic and life situations.

SUMMARY

This chapter presented a wide variety of strategies aimed at managing risk for primary school grades. Further, this chapter provided criteria for the development of a comprehensive curriculum that actually teaches life skills and promotes student well-being.

Through understanding and use of the curriculum and instructional strategies developed in this chapter, it is hoped that elementary schools will be more cognizant of their role in the prevention of and programming for high-risk students.

CHAPTER 3

Student Assistance: Grades K–4

Many youngsters lack the necessary life skills and/or family support structures to help them through difficult times. Growing up without adequate life skills and needed assistance typically creates major developmental problems for these youngsters. Often these problems manifest themselves in:

— low self-esteem
— an inability to make rational decisions, usually following a pleasure seeking pattern while lacking sound information as a basis for decisions
— an inability to cope with the pressures of home, school, and relationships often developing avoidance or other dysfunctional behavior
— high absenteeism
— complaints of illness and request to go the nurse
— excessive daydreaming
— unwillingness to work on group tasks in the classroom
— avoidance of other students during play periods
— changed behavior
— low achievement
— acting-out behaviors

Not all children are at equal risk of becoming disaffected with school. Some of the groups of students who may be at high risk are:

— students undergoing trauma in the home such as the death of a family member, divorce or separation, abuse, neglect
— students who are new to the school or who have moved frequently
— students who have lags in academic skill development
— students who have been retained
— students who receive atypical school services such as remedial instruction through "pull out" programs, mainstreamed

special education students, students with limited English speaking ability and certain gifted students

Obviously, schools and individual teachers cannot control all the variables and outside influences that interfere with a child's ability to learn. However, by having a formal mechanism to identify, program, and monitor high-risk students, schools can help prevent the long-term effects of life crises.

Student assistance includes all the planned and spontaneous ways schools attempt to assist high-risk youngsters. Planned intervention can include formal interviews by guidance counselors, school psychologists or referrals to outside social service agencies. Informal intervention activities can include additional academic assistance, help in establishing friendships among students, or simply provision of needed emotional support during times of crises.

TEAM APPROACH TO MANAGING RISK

A student assistance team composed of an administrator, school nurse and several teachers can be established. Annually, all teachers can assess the students in their class in terms of learning-distractive behavior. The individual teacher can use the information to focus on the children currently enrolled in his/her class. The student assistance team can look for patterns of behavior or high-risk situations which may interfere with a child's ability to reach his/her potential.

Some of the specific actions that can be initiated by this team include, but are not limited to:

— Modifying the student's program so that the child meets with more success
— Providing more large group activities, such as in-common reading, so the students in the low reading groups work regularly with the total class
— Changing the physical arrangement of the class so that certain students can be separated or encouraged to work together
— Avoiding classroom activities which emphasize success and failure. The spelling bee is such an activity. Those that most need help in spelling are excluded first, so learning is minimized, and as children are eliminated their failure is made public.

— Providing an ongoing support system for teachers to explore problem-solving techniques

How it Works—A Case Study
Elementary Student Assistance Team

Bobby is referred to the student assistance team by his classroom teacher. Essentially, the teacher is concerned with the child's lack of enthusiasm toward school, his declining attention to his personal appearance and his lack of stable relationships with his classmates. The teacher, Mrs. Phillips, believes that these behaviors have had a direct effect on Bobby's poor academic achievement and feeling of alienation.

The team begins by collecting data concerning family history, academic record and by interviewing staff members who have contact with Bobby. The school nurse reviews all health records and meets with Bobby to get a basic perception of his physical well-being. The principal reviews all academic records. The classroom teacher begins systematically to document behaviors to support the initial concerns.

The team meets to review the information and concludes that Bobby's parents should be asked to attend a meeting of the team to develop a plan of action. At this meeting a recommended plan is discussed, specific expectations for Bobby, his parents and school are developed, and timelines for ongoing feedback and assessment are established, specifically:

- The principal will maintain a position of advocacy by monitoring Bobby's progress on a daily basis. Further, he will meet with Bobby twice a week to develop an ongoing relationship and to provide a vehicle to facilitate Bobby's communication, decision-making and interpersonal skills. Finally, the principal will provide a list of school and community related after-school activities that the parents can choose as a means to encourage a linkage with Bobby's peers that will hopefully lead to meaningful friendships.

- The nurse will meet with Bobby on a monthly basis to monitor physical well-being and attendance. Further, the nurse will look for any indications of family neglect.

- The classroom teacher will continue to monitor both academic and emotional well-being. Specifically, Bobby will be placed in more cooperative team-learning situations; the child will be given a leadership role in various recess activities; a peer-tutoring relationship with a positive role model from a higher grade will be established; and Mrs. Phillips will meet with Bobby at the end of the school day to organize homework assignments, review the day's activities and respond to positive behaviors.

- Bobby's parents will provide active support and commitment to the plan by attending weekly conferences during the next month; by insuring that Bobby has a positive climate at home to complete school work; by carefully monitoring Bobby's social development and actively engage him in healthy after-school activities; by encouraging positive peer relationships by inviting classmates home; by reinforcing the importance of personal care and its impact on self-esteem.

This team approach establishes an ongoing way to identify students with high risk potential. It is to be looked upon as an intervention, not a treatment program. This type of program provides a way for school officials to help students, enlighten parents, and maintain a vehicle for professional support among staff members.

CHILDHOOD CRISES/SPECIFIC AT-RISK GROUPS

Not all school days or experiences have equal impact on a child. Looking back at your own school days certain experiences stand out—the trip to the zoo, being unjustly accused of misbehavior, the one-to-one talk you had with a teacher. Since all days are not equal in terms of long-range impact special activities need not be planned every day to try and motivate a child who shows signs of disaffection. In some cases the causes of the behavior are short-lived, for example, a family situation, a fight with friends, a poor report card.

The entire elementary school experience of the child should be viewed as contributing to maximizing learning and reducing risk. Research consistently shows that children who exhibit certain behaviors are at particular risk (Rutter, 1980). The school has many opportunities to reduce these risks. A major attribute of many children at risk is poor academic achievement. Everything the school does to reduce failure or perceived failure can also be considered part of the prevention program. At-risk children frequently come from homes with inconsistent expectations and discipline. The consistency of school procedures, schedules, and expecta-

Elementary School
Student Assistance Program Organization

REFERRAL

(Parent, School Personnel, Student Self-referral, Outside Agency)

STUDENT ASSISTANCE TEAM

(Determine Risk)

TEAM MEMBER ASSIGNED

Parent Contacted

Mentorship		
Ongoing Instruction Strategies		
Counselling		
Peer Leadership		
Special Education Team		
Internal Intervention		
Crisis Intervention		
Agency Referral		

tions can offset, at least to a degree the home environment. Children at risk often have trouble with peer relationships. There are many opportunities for the school to assist students in developing positive relationships. Children at risk frequently do not "like" school and feel they do not belong. Schools can create an environment of inclusion which will minimize alienation. By being aware of problems affecting the child and taking direct action the teacher can increase learning and reduce the risk of destructive behavior.

Family Separation, Divorce, Remarriage or Death

Today with the number of families undergoing divorces and remarriages, students have personal crises to deal with in addition to more traditional traumas such as death and dying. How the teacher handles these situations can have both short- and long-term effects on the child's attitude toward school and learning. The symptoms displayed by children in the classroom may be very similar in the case of divorce and in the case of a death in the family. However, in the case of death in the family, the school is usually notified immediately. In the case of divorce, symptoms may appear when there is separation or even when the child is told that one parent will be moving. In some cases the child will also be moving. Boys frequently respond more strongly to divorce than girls; however, temperament, parental response, past experience, reactions of friends and teachers also influence the child's response.

Some of the symptoms a child may display at times of crises are:

— changes in the way the child is dressed
— outbursts of crying or anger
— lateness to school
— complaints of illness, such as headaches or stomachaches

Sometimes a child may suddenly become overly interested in perfection in school and be upset by a low grade on a test. These cases may be harder to spot, but may indicate a child who thinks that if he is "good enough" the family situation will go back to normal. Older children in the family may also exhibit this kind of behavior because they feel they are responsible for brothers and sisters.

Some of the ways teachers can help children during these times of high stress are:

— Let the child know that you recognize the pain. If the child cries, say something like "You are hurting inside" or "You feel all alone, don't you?"

- Let the child talk about the problem. Be a good listener; you do not need to give advice. Just be supportive and show you care.
- Provide extra reinforcement to show that you value the child, "I am glad to see you in school today."
- While it is important to be supportive it is also important to maintain routine for the child. Specifically, when the child's world is in upheaval he needs to be able to count on the stability of the classroom. Classroom rules and discipline should be enforced and children should participate in regular activities.
- Be sensitive to the subject content in the class. If you read to students, you may want to avoid a story that deals with the joys of a typical (mother, father, two child) happy family. Remember the "typical family" is less than 17% of families. If you can't avoid this kind of topic, discuss other kinds of family groups. Remember one child may be in a crisis period, but many of your children probably come from non-traditional families.
- Keep your expectations for the child high. Don't fall into the trap of thinking or saying, "What can you expect of Johnny with his family problems?" You may have to balance your expectations against real events, such as failure to do homework, for a short time, but you should expect it to be a short period.
- Prejudice should be avoided. Single family homes can be supportive and the children from such homes successful. In some cases where there has been much fighting or even abuse the new home situation may be more supportive for the child.
- Don't betray confidences. Things that the child tells you should not be passed on to colleagues. An exception is when the information indicates a danger to the child or another person. For example, child abuse must be reported.

Latch-Key Children

The traditional family of mother, father and children, where the father works and the mother stays home, no longer can be considered the typical family structure. In most communities only a few of the children in the classroom will come from the "traditional" home. Further, family structures which include only one parent living in the home are commonplace. Since most elementary teachers are women with families they will also be functioning in "non-traditional" families. A major concern in single-parent families or in two-working-parent families is care of the children when school is not in session. Even when finances are adequate, finding adequate daycare can be a problem. When finances are very limited, which could be the case in many single-parent families, daycare becomes a continuing crisis. In many communities the pressure for full-day kindergarten is more motivated by the need for daycare than by educational concerns.

While public schools do not have a legal responsibility for providing before- and after-school care, facilitating daycare programs will have direct academic payoffs in the classroom. Tension in the home caused by patched together or sporadic before- and after-school care is carried into the classroom by the child. Schools can help to minimize the problems associated with before- and after-school care to varying degrees and by means such as the following.

LISTS OF SERVICES

A simple but helpful way for schools to help parents deal with the before-/after-school care problem is by maintaining lists of daycare centers and individuals who provide services. The school should make it clear that they are not recommending any of these services. However, such a list can be very valuable to new parents in the community, parents who, because of changes in the family, must seek daycare and to parents who must change daycare arrangements. The development and maintainance of the list could be a project of the PTA. The directory idea could be enhanced by listing a parent who currently uses the service and would be willing to talk to other parents.

ASSISTING IN PROVISION OF SERVICES

Many schools today have empty rooms and some districts have empty schools which can be rented to either private or nonprofit child care centers. Rental prices can be set to help maintain a reasonable cost of the services. Specifications for the services to be provided and cost limits can be combined with bidding to allow for alternative proposals. Nonprofit groups in the community such as churches, synagogues, and YMCAs can be actively encouraged to provide services for children before and after school.

Transportation is another area in which schools can actively facilitate quality before- and after-school care. The Board of Education, depending on state laws, may be able to set policies that allow students who are bused to school anyway to be picked up or dropped off at daycare centers. Provisions can also be made to charge parents for transportation beyond that provided normally by the district.

For example, in a district with three elementary schools, a preschool/before- and after-school program is run by a daycare specialist in rooms rented in one elementary school. The district school buses pick students up from the program before school and take them to the child's regular school. The buses take the children in the after-school program to the program at the end of the school day. The parents pay the daycare center for the program and the district on a cost-per-mile basis for the transportation.

PROVIDING BEFORE-/AFTER-SCHOOL CARE

Another approach for providing before/after-school care is for the school district to directly provide the service. The services can be provided free or on a fee basis. State laws may affect how this might best be done. Interesting to note is that, even if the service were provided free at the elementary level, it is unlikely that it would cost nearly as much as the high school after-school athletic program.

A before-/after-school program can be provided with no additional facilities by using the regular classrooms and all-purpose room. However, provisions must be made to have the rooms ready for regular school instruction at the appropriate time. It is helpful if there is at least one room dedicated to the before-/after-school program where materials and supplies can be stored.

Teachers and aides for the program can be hired by the district directly. Some teachers may welcome the opportunity to earn extra income by taking part in the before- or after-school section of the program. Another option is to issue a contract to a daycare service to provide staff for the program.

One district which has run a before-/after-school program for years, provides services in each elementary school. Parents can drop children off at 7:00 A.M. and pick them up as late as 6:00 P.M. Teachers in the district provide the program and are paid extra for the additional time. Senior citizens act as volunteer aids in the program.

New Students

Even in very stable communities new students can be expected to enter the school throughout the year. A procedure should be established for incorporating new students into the school society. It is not enough to just determine the students' instructional level; the expectations of the school and classroom must also be communicated. Transferring schools is a difficult experience for a child. If he/she knows how things are run and what is expected in this new place, then stress will be reduced. On the other hand, it is also important for maintaining the norms of the school, that new students coming from schools with less positive norms not become role models for your students.

Parents of new students also need to know what the expectations of the new school are and how to communicate with the principal and teacher. There should be a standard packet of information, and, if possible, a conference with the teacher or principal.

Handicapped Children

Estimates indicate that as many as 10 to 15 percent of all children may have a handicapping condition which requires special education (Hasazi, 1979). Today the law requires that these children be educated in the "least restrictive environment" (Public Law 94-142, The Education for All Handicapped Children Act). This means that the child should be educated with nonhandicapped children in the regular classroom whenever possible. More severely handicapped children should be educated in combinations of regular and self-contained environments. Even severely handicapped children should be retained within the school in self-contained classes, whenever possible, rather than in institutions or special schools.

Classroom teachers are directly involved in identifying children with handicapping conditions, planning their programs and teaching these children at least part-time in their classes. The teacher's attitude and knowledge vis-a-vis the handicapping condition and the child with these conditions will affect the adjustment and the achievement of the child.

IDENTIFICATION

The higher the grade you teach the more apt you are as a teacher to have children in your class who have been previously identified as needing special education in your class. However, there will continue to be students who have exceptional needs which have to be identified and provided with special services and/or programs.

All classrooms have wide ranges in terms of ability, past learning and attitudes. However, in most cases through planning and adapting materials, pace of instruction and approach to instruction, the needs of students can be accommodated. Teachers must be careful, particularly in the early grades, that normal differences in rates of maturing or limited previous learning opportunities are not confused with handicapping conditions requiring special programs. It is of concern that even within a school there are frequently marked differences in the number of "referrals" for special education generated by different teachers. In schools where the children come from social and economic backgrounds different from their teachers there tend to be more referrals (Henley, 1985). Teachers and principals must guard against over-identification. Teachers should realize that referring a student does not reduce their responsibility to teach the child. Too frequently you hear a teacher say "I referred Johnny two months ago and after all the testing and meeting, he is still in my class. All I got out of it were some suggestions on how I could handle Johnny in my class. That special education assessment team is useless." The problem is in expectations. The teacher thought the child study team would assume responsibility for "Johnny" and the child study team viewed its role as helping the teacher assume the teaching responsibility for "Johnny."

While there are dangers in over-identification, there are also dangers in not recognizing the needs of children which go beyond what the teacher can provide. Districts have procedures for identifying, referring and assessing students. Checklists are typically provided to assist teachers in identification; however, the principal and special education staff need to provide specific training to help classroom teachers.

The attitude of the teacher toward the handicapped child is terribly important. Not only will the attitude affect what the student learns academically but will affect how the other students in the class react to the student. In some cases the teacher is "afraid" of the student. Not a physical fear but a fear of not being able to predict or control behavior, fear that they will "do something wrong" and hurt the child's feeling or fear that they just don't know enough to teach this child and the rest of the class at the same time. In some cases the teacher just doesn't think "these" children should be the regular teacher's responsibility. It is the law (94-142), and it is the teacher's obligation to comply. It is the principal's responsibility to ensure compliance. However, the classroom teacher is only one member of a team of professionals who share responsibility for the education of the child. The teacher needs and should seek the assistance of the other members of the team in planning and carrying out the program. Following is a list of a few ways teachers can foster learning in a mainstreamed environment:

— The teacher can discuss the child's specific strengths and problems with the child study team, or, if the child spends part of the day in a resource room or self-contained class with the special education teacher. The individual education plan (IEP) is a one-year plan, which sets direction for classroom learning but is not designed to be a day-by-day lesson plan. Specific information concerning motivation, learning style, level of instruction, social interaction with peers, classroom behavior, parent involvement and in some cases physical needs or limitations is needed.

The strategies listed below can be used to help maximize learning for the handicapped child:

— The teacher should set a few specific short-range objectives (a week, a month).
— Specific strategies for achieving the objectives should then be developed.
— The teacher should let the child know what the objectives are and how both teacher and child will know when the objectives have been achieved.
— Handicapped children need structured variety, not just drill and practice. Manipulative materials can assist in developing understanding. Peer tutoring can also be productive, and not just with the handicapped child being tutored. The handicapped child also has strengths and can work with other children, in the class or with a child in a lower grade.
— Behavior problems can affect the entire class and the handicapped child. Not all handicapped children are hyperactive or disruptive. However, when behavior negatively affects the learning of the child or others in the class, a specific plan to modify the child's action needs to be developed. Specific objectives need to be set, "Johnny will reduce by ninety percent the times he calls out without raising his hand." A reward structure can be established. When he raises his hand he can earn praise or even points toward doing a special activity. Analyzing when a negative behavior occurs can also be helpful. The negative behaviors may come near the end of an activity indicating the child has reached the end of his attention span. Shortening the activity for the child may reduce the problem.

- Some handicapped children are very shy and withdrawn. In these cases specific objectives need to be set and activities planned to get the handicapped involved in the class, on the playground, and with their peers. Building trust with such children is particularly important. Provide small opportunities for success and praise, and avoid embarrassing the child.
- Parents can be very helpful in planning and supporting specific learning plans. They frequently know what motivates their child and what causes negative reactions. If they know what you are trying to accomplish with their child they can continue the support at home.

Gifted Children

Linda Silverman defines the gifted child as "one who is developmentally advanced in one or more areas, and is therefore in need of differentiated programs in order to develop at his or her own accelerated pace" (in Maker, 1986, p. 58). Most research concludes that "differentiation of program" should include acceleration of content learning and opportunities to study in-depth ideas, use higher level thinking skills and use specialized resources. Failure to provide for the learning needs of gifted students can lead to boredom and disinterest in school.

Not all gifted children are straight-"A" students in all subjects. Students may be gifted in math but not language. Others, even young children, may have already decided that being "smart" makes them lonely. Such a child may become the quiet child, who weakly says "I don't know," when asked a question. On the other hand, the child may act out in class and not pay attention to the lesson. These children need to be identified and have their teacher and peers accept their abilities.

Acceleration of gifted students by skipping grades can cause problems if not carefully managed. In the first place, merely putting a student in a higher grade, while allowing for some vertical movement in content will not automatically mean he/she will have opportunities for in-depth and higher order learning. Program in both the current class and proposed accelerated placement must be analyzed and matched to the student's needs. Another factor which must be considered is the student's peer relationships. Will grade acceleration put the child at a disadvantage in interacting with other children? Does he/she play with older children? Can he/she physically compete with older children on the playground?

Parents frequently request early admission to kindergarten for children who have some reading skills or other demonstrated academic skills. These requests should be carefully considered by the school. The child's intellectual, physical, social and emotional readiness for kindergarten should each be assessed in light of the program offered by the school. For example, a child may already have mastered some academic skills, but if he/she is too immature to direct his/her focus on tasks for a sustained period of time he/she may not be ready for an academic kindergarten.

Gifted students can be maintained with their age peers in most cases. Provisions can be made in the classroom for acceleration and in-depth exploration of content. Students can be assigned to higher grade classes for part of the day's instruction or assigned a mentor. A couple of gifted students can be assigned to the same class so that they can work with intellectual peers. In cases where the child is "profoundly" gifted, it may be necessary for the school staff to develop a formal individual educational plan (IEP). Parents, teachers, school psychologist and possibly the child should develop the plan. Ideally, the child would spend part of the school day working with intellectual peers and part of the day working with age peers.

The following should be considered:

- Gifted students, whether accelerated or not, can have peer problems. Teachers can help children deal effectively with the problems.
- Students can be assigned to work in pairs for part of the day. The pairings can be designed to put two gifted students together or to foster interaction with non-gifted peers.
- The teacher should avoid making the gifted child appear different or strange to other children in the class. For example, always calling on the child when other students fail to answer a question.
- If the student is assigned part of the day to another classroom or if the school has a program for gifted students which the child attends part of the day, the teacher should make the child feel comfortable about leaving and re-entering the classroom. Work missed in the classroom should be made up by the child only to the degree necessary to learn the material missed. The gifted child may need to do only five problems where other children may need to do twenty-five. Leaving the classroom to attend another program is not a reward for good behavior, it is a program to meet a need. Some children

become anxious or feel they are being punished if they have to do twice the work or miss the "fun" activities in the regular classroom.
- The teacher can provide direct help to the student with peer problems by teaching group interaction skills and designing situations where students can practice these skills, i.e., science or social studies projects.
- Some gifted students may not have the skills or coordination to play effectively with other children. The child may need tutoring in these skills as much as he/she needs accelerated math content.

Non-English-Speaking Children

It is likely that a classroom teacher will have a non-English-speaking student placed in the classroom. Schools on the East and West coasts sometimes report that they are serving students who speak thirty different languages. Having a foreign non-English-speaking child in your classroom can be a real learning experience for the other children in the class. It is often amazing how quickly children learn English in a supportive environment. One does not have to be a language teacher to provide a learning environment for the English-as-a-second-language (ESL) child.

The first priority for the child is to learn English. Don't worry about having the child "keep up" in all the various subjects. The child may be able to use the math book or do board work in math very quickly but is not likely to understand much of the textbook in history. Don't try and force the child into a basal reader before he/she has sight vocabulary.

If there is someone else in the school who speaks the same language as the child they can be helpful in determining the academic level the child achieved in his native country, as well as some of the interests of the child. However, such a resource person should not serve as a crutch for the child. There should be someone who speaks the child's language identified in case of an emergency; the child's parents or some other relative may speak English; the foreign language department in the high school may be able to help; or a social services agency or a local college.

Following are some of the ways the classroom teacher can assist the ESL child:

- If you know in advance that an ESL child is assigned to your class, prepare the other children in advance. Aim to have the class see the entrance of the student as a positive experience, an adventure. Use a map and show the children where the child's country is. Show a film or read a story about the country.

— Discuss with the class what the new child will need to know about the school. Make a list: "Where the cafeteria is." "Where the restroom is." "Where to put his coat." The children can discuss how they can communicate these things to the child.

— Assign a "special friend" to the child. Maybe a child who lives near the newcomer or one who has similar interests. Have the child accompany the ESL child through the daily routine of the class and school. Take the student on a tour of the school pointing out the cafeteria, nurse's office, art room, office, and playground.

— Use as many visuals in the classroom as possible. Film strips, movies, flash cards, graphs, and maps can all be useful. Tape stories and have the child listen and follow the story in the book. Computers can also be of help in building sight vocabulary. Voice synthesizers can be added to computers and allow the child to hear what he types. Television programs such as "Sesame Street" and the "Electric Company" can be helpful.

— Obtain a bilingual dictionary in English and the native language. This can be used as a reference manual for you and the student.

— Have the students make labels and attach them to various items in the room.

— The ESL child can benefit from individual or small group instruction which exposes him/her to the language. Classes in basic skills, either funded locally or under Chapter I, may be helpful. The speech therapist may also be of assistance to the child in the area of articulation. Parent volunteers or aides may provide additional one-on-one support.

SUMMARY

This chapter introduced the concept of a Student Assistance Team as a vehicle to identify and develop programs for high-risk students. Additionally, strategies for assisting potentially high-risk students within the elementary school were discussed.

Careful recognition of these potentially high-risk groups, as well as the establishment of a team approach to manage risk, should prove beneficial to all schools which are willing to enrich their primary prevention role. Further, those processes related to a student assistance team can be expanded throughout a school district.

Concepts related to the development and maintenance of student assistance teams at all grade levels will be presented in subsequent chapters.

CHAPTER 4

Managing Risks to
Maximize Learning: Grades 5–8

It is important to note that teaching behaviors related to school effectiveness characteristics are applicable at all grade levels. Thus, those concepts discussed in the previous chapters of this book should be reviewed and can be implemented within schools. It is of special importance that middle school teachers focus on climate factors in their classrooms. There is often a feeling among "upper grade" teachers that climate is an elementary school concept that has diminished relevance in junior and secondary schools. Many teachers of these grade levels are committed to their subject first and to the concepts related to teaching and climate secondly.

Based on a variety of social and emotional needs of upper grade students, there is growing support for the notion that as a student progresses in grade level, climate becomes more important for achievement. Thus, the establishment of a healthy school and classroom climate in the middle grades continues to be a significant prerequisite to ensuring student well-being. The specific characteristics of the early adolescent such as rapid growth, sexual maturity, self-consciousness, heightened need for peer approval and emotional stability make it necessary for middle/junior high level schools to develop programs and procedures that are uniquely tailored to their students. Although the general characteristics of effective schools can and should be used to guide school practices, it is important that recognition of the physical, social and emotional needs associated with the early adolescent become a cornerstone for program planning.

This chapter will present a variety of school programs and practices that will help develop and maintain positive school norms. Additionally, as in the previous chapter, specific models for curriculum planning, identification of high-risk students, establishment of a team approach to addressing the needs of potential high-risk students, intervention strategies, and community and social service agency networking will be explored.

DEVELOPMENT AND MAINTENANCE OF SCHOOL NORMS

The imposing self-consciousness associated with early adolescence leads children to group together and to develop somewhat short-lived, yet intense relationships. These relationships are usually established around similarities in tastes for music, clothing, leisure-time activities, etc. In many cases, the approval of friends becomes more important than that of parents or teachers.

Based on this phenomenon, it is absolutely essential that middle/junior schools establish and clearly communicate school standards and expectations. These standards should represent an understanding of peer influence and provide specific information to assist students in making choices when confronted with negative peer relations.

There are many ways in which schools can exert positive influences on the behavior of their students. All who work and study within the school must be encouraged to take an active role in shaping school norms.

There is a consistent relationship between school environments and students' feelings and behavior in them (Strother, 1983). Adolescents tend to respond more positively when the school setting provides clear expectations for behavior, when they or their peers have participated in defining behavioral rules, when all persons in the school setting show sensitivity to individuals, and when all rules are fairly and consistently enforced.

A Phi Delta Kappa study (Wayson & Lasely, 1984) identified several characteristics of schools that were effective in fostering student self-discipline and acceptance of established norms. The schools:

– created student "belongingness" and responsibility
– established and pursued long-range and comprehensive goals
– created symbols of identity and excellence
– fostered student leadership to sustain positive school values
– created clear formal and informal rules, which were
  understood by the students

Matriello (1984) has identified a quality of "spirit" or "common culture" within such schools. In these schools the emphasis is on expectations, not on lists of specific rules with penalties for noncompliance.

Student Job Description

I get enough sleep.
I eat a nutritious breakfast.
I attend school regularly.   **GRADES 4–8**
I arrive at school on time.
I arrive at classes on time.
I have a positive attitude toward school and my schoolwork.
I treat my teacher(s) with respect.
I accept responsibility for all my actions.
I do my best to complete all my classwork.
I have a special study place at home away from the phone,
  TV and other distractions.
I complete my homework and return it to school when done.
I avoid situations where other students are not conforming
  to school rules.
I discuss my schoolwork and any problems I have at school
  with my parents.

The most obvious (and probably the best) place to start establishing sets of norms is in THE VERY EARLY STAGES, shortly before students enter the middle/junior school. Holding student and parent meetings at the sending elementary schools provides a vehicle to communicate school goals, expectations and various operational procedures. It is at this time that students and parents should become familiar with the school's Student Job Description.

This job description, like the one cited in Chapter 2, should clearly outline the role expectation for all students and provide a basis to help shape school norms. Further, students should be given an opportunity to visit their soon-to-be school to view, firsthand, how the school operates and to help them to minimize the anxieties associated with moving away from a self-contained classroom setting to one that is organized either for team or departmentalized instructional units.

It is important that these incoming students have the opportunity to visit with successful upper grade students in the school. The initial impression of a positive role model will help provide a successful orientation toward the school and help legitimize established school norms.

Upon the students' formal arrival in the middle/junior high school, norms and expectations should be reviewed. This discussion should include an explanation concerning the collaborative nature of the norms, the behavioral expectations associated with the norms and the process by which existing norms/rules can be challenged. It is again very important that student leaders are involved in these activities. Further, if at all possible, ongoing interaction groups composed of newly arrived students, positive role model upper grade students, and a guidance counselor (or other trained facilitator) should be developed to ensure the maintenance of existing norms and provide a vehicle for discussing school values and goals.

These groups should not be purely problem finding or problem solving in nature; instead they should provide a focus toward the common good and provide a vehicle for younger students to integrate into the greater school environment.

The fundamental expectation for students is that they will become able to control and direct their own behavior. From this basic expectation, it becomes the school's role to structure activities and social interaction which will foster behaviors towards a pre-established notion of norms and shared responsibilities.

CURRICULUM TO REDUCE RISK, GRADES 5–8

A student wellness curriculum must be planned with awareness of those conditions which have relevance for personal health. Content and learning experiences should be selected to enable students to make intelligent and informed decisions in areas which affect their health and well-being. Specifically, concepts related to personal growth, fitness and health, and drugs and mental health should provide the basic initiatives for program planning.

Personal Growth

By understanding the functions of his/her body, a student of middle/junior school age can better deal with the stresses related to the psychological changes of that period. Students should be taught to identify and understand the physical, emotional and social characteristics of adolescence. Further, information regarding human reproduction, the birth process, and human growth and development should be taught so that each student can better understand and develop pride in his/her growing body and build a wholesome attitude toward sex.

Strategies to help deal with social stressors related to dating, peer pressure, academics and a variety of family conflicts that are common to adolescence should be taught. Additionally, instructional strategies such as simulation, role play, and group problem solving should be emphasized so that students can develop needed decision-making and social interaction skills.

Fitness and Health

Students need to be aware that while all persons grow and develop similarly, individual patterns and personal needs vary in terms of bodily systems, functions and growth. Concepts related to nutrition, sleep and physical activity should be linked to personal growth and well-being. Specific nutritional disorders such as anorexia and bulimia should be discussed so that students can identify the external as well as the internal influences on dietary tastes.

In summary, students must be taught to understand the important interrelationships among the physical, emotional and social aspects of growing up.

Drugs and Mental Health

The need for drug education becomes increasingly significant during a student's middle/junior high school years. The stressors of adolescence, the increasing reliance on peer approval, the availability of drugs, the impact of media and music, and the growing need for independence all provide environmental and developmental potential for experimentation with drugs and alcohol. Although the primary objective of a drug program is to aid in the prevention of drug abuse, concepts related to the development of individual standards, critical thinking, decision-making, interpersonal relations, stress reduction, communication and self-esteem should also play a major role in program planning.

This brief discussion involving curriculum development is meant to provide a broad-based outline of the kinds of topics that should be included in a middle/junior high school health/student wellness curriculum. Obviously, the scope and breadth of a school's program will depend on an assessment of need, the availability of resources and the recognition of local standards and expectations.

Scope and Sequence

"Here's Looking At You, 2000" presents drug-related issues in a comprehensive manner from kindergarten through twelfth grade. The curriculum was developed so that students could progress through school learning new information and skills while reviewing old ones. Thus, most of the topics are reinforced in succeeding grades, with students' exposure to the topic becoming wider and deeper. The following chart, based on the objectives for each lesson, illustrates the scope of topics and the sequence in which they are presented.

Information	5	6	7–9
dangers of unknown substances			
drugs and their effects	X	X	X
definition of drug	X	X	X
chemical dependency and the individual	X		
chemical dependency in the family		X	X
alcohol	X	X	X
nicotine	X	X	X
marijuana	X	X	X
look-alike stimulants			X
cocaine			
other drugs			
reasons why people use and don't use drugs			X
risk factors and ways to reduce risks	X		X
identification and evaluation of sources of information about drugs		X	X
drug advertisements		X	X
drugs causing problems in future as well as in present		X	
factors which influence effects			X
non-stereotypical description of drug users			X
basic properties of cancer cells			X
fetal alcohol syndrome			X
abusers hurting others			X
driving and drugs			X
sidestream smoke			
drug-related emergencies			
control of substances by federal schedules			
sexuality and drugs			
early warning signs of drug abuse			
action on drug-related issues			

Skills	5	6	7–9
asking someone for something			
abiding by ground rules for discussing sensitive topics in front of others	X	X	X
making decisions	X	X	X
asking someone to do something (assertiveness)			
keeping out of trouble (self-control)			
identifying sources of influence			
saying no to keep friends	X	X	X

(continued)

Skills *(continued)*	5	6	7–9
making friends		X	X
stopping enabling			
intervening with friends			
recognizing when to refer people to others			
making referrals			
teaching refusal skills			

Bonding to School and Family	5	6	7–9
explaining that problems are normal			
acknowledging feelings and dealing with them			
helping others feel included			
appreciating self as special	X	X	X
identifying ways to take care of the body			
identifying healthy ways to have fun	X	X	X
identifying personal strengths		X	X
identifying others' strengths		X	X
identifying sources of self-assessment	X		
assessing self	X		
recognizing power of saying no	X		
recognizing the influence of stress	X		
identifying stressful situations and dealing with them	X		
asking for advice from a trusted person	X		
giving positive self-talk	X		X
giving affirmations to others	X		X
identifying what is important to self		X	
learning what is important to others		X	
identifying and building relationship with someone admired		X	
getting feedback about personal qualities		X	
understanding group pressures		X	
discussing adolescent concerns			X
identifying feelings about drugs, dependency			
responding to people without using stereotypes			

STUDENT ASSISTANCE, GRADES 5–8

The dynamics of "growing up" compounded by the influences of the media and peers provide a genuine basis for potential dysfunctional behavior for middle/junior high school students. Despite efforts to establish and reinforce positive school norms and provide a curriculum that specifically addresses a wide variety of socio-emotional issues, it is still highly likely that a portion of the school population will be unable to take full advantage of the academic, social and athletic opportunities available in the school.

The school must initiate a formal mechanism to identify these students, to insure parental support in the early stages of intervention and to monitor the ongoing effectiveness of remediation strategies. Establishment of a student assistance team, made up of concerned, skilled professional staff members, can serve as a formal, ongoing vehicle for these purposes.

It is again important to note that this team should not replace a child study team whose role is to diagnose specific learning or emotional disabilities. Nor should this team assume the role of therapist in its dealings with high-risk students. Instead, its purpose is to serve the role of child advocate by identifying potentially high-risk students, collecting data to support this assumption, sharing the information with parents, developing an intervention strategy to help the child be more successful in school, and providing the parent with a network of social service agencies that can help to deal with those student-related problems (such as severe depression, socially maladjusted behaviors, substance abuse, etc.) that are simply too complex for the school to deal with by itself.

Identifying High-Risk Students

School personnel must provide a mechanism to identify types of children who are "at risk" for dysfunctional behavior. This becomes increasingly important for those staff members working in the middle/junior high grade levels since much research points to these grades as the most likely time a child will begin to shape his/her social group preferences and experiment with drugs and alcohol (Roberts, 1986). School personnel must be able to identify children whose social, school, or family situations make them more likely to become dissatisfied with themselves and therefore, have greater potential to turn to dysfunctional means to satisfy their developmental needs.

The following list provides an overview of those student characteristics most closely associated with high-risk behavior and early use of drugs (Roberts, 1986):

− The child does poorly in school.
− The child is unable to get along with others.
− The child's peers, or older children they play with, use drugs.
− Someone in the child's home has a drug problem.
− The child does not like school, and feels as if he/she doesn't belong there.
− Rules and discipline in the home are unclear and inconsistent.
− The child continually resists authority.

It is important that teachers and administrators become familiar with these characteristics and are sensitized to the need for taking a proactive role in the identification of those students who are most likely to exhibit potential for dysfunctional behaviors. As school personnel carefully plan teaching activities to promote specific academic proficiencies, they must also plan for early identification and remediation of high-risk students.

The Role of the Student Assistance Team

It is essential that as students reach the intermediate grades there is a systematic effort to assess each student's potential for dysfunctional and/or destructive behavior. This assessment should be undertaken by the teachers in an entire grade level. The assessment itself should focus on those characteristics that have a high correlation to poor achievement, dissatisfaction with school, alienation and other high-risk student behaviors.

An analysis of such a survey will:

— force teachers to make an early assessment of potential student problems
— provide the basis for more in-depth study of individual students
— establish a benchmark by which strategies for intervention can be initiated

As the list of disaffected students is carefully studied, it will become somewhat obvious that several students are in significant danger of both academic and life-related failure. It is important that a more detailed investigation of the behavioral characteristics of these students be carefully attended to. Thus, all school personnel who have contact with these now identified high-risk students must provide more specific information regarding the child's behavioral patterns, social interaction, academic progress, physical well-being, etc. To identify disaffected students, the checklist on the following page has been developed.

Concurrently, the members of the Student Assistance Team begin to collect other pertinent information that will help establish a behavioral student profile and provide a framework to help shape intervention strategies.

Typically, the members of the Student Assistance Team should include the school principal (or other administrative personnel), the school nurse or guidance counselor, and several interested teachers. Although the exact make-up of the group may differ by choice, it is important to include staff members who have a consid-

Please place this in a sealed envelope to ensure confidentiality.

Student _____ Date _____

School _____ Teacher _____

Please return to _____

Please CHECK the behaviors that this student is exhibiting which are a cause of concern to you.
Please CIRCLE non-acceptable behavior frequency: 1) often; 2) sometimes; 3) occasionally.

Behavior	Frequency			
Personal habits have changed (dress, shaving, hair, bathing; disinterest)	☐	1	2	3
Personality has changed (obviously)	☐	1	2	3
Physical complaints (frequent visits to nurse, stomachaches, headaches, etc.)	☐	1	2	3
Blames other people, places, things for his/her difficulty	☐	1	2	3
Inconsistent in aggressiveness/passivity in classroom participation	☐	1	2	3
Falls asleep in class	☐	1	2	3
Has difficulty concentrating in class	☐	1	2	3
Excessively quiet and withdrawn/nervous, depressed	☐	1	2	3
Displays dramatic attention-getting tactics, such as _____	☐	1	2	3
Does not comply with school regulations (general trouble in school)	☐	1	2	3
Continually late for class/school	☐	1	2	3
High rate of absenteeism	☐	1	2	3
Grades are inconsistent and/or dropping off	☐	1	2	3
Difficulty completing tasks or assignments	☐	1	2	3
Works below potential level	☐	1	2	3
Avoids close peer relationships or a change in peer group affiliations	☐	1	2	3
Inconsistent over-achiever	☐	1	2	3
Seeks approval and may become excessively hurt, agitated or worried if not granted	☐	1	2	3
Difficulty separating from home	☐	1	2	3
Lack of interest (as compared to prior interest)	☐	1	2	3
Fighting with peers and throwing temper tantrums	☐	1	2	3
Lying	☐	1	2	3
Difficulty socializing with peers	☐	1	2	3
Has bruises	☐	1	2	3
A compulsive clown	☐	1	2	3
Becomes extremely upset when school work is less than perfect	☐	1	2	3
Becomes tense at end of the day before going home	☐	1	2	3

Additional Comments: _____

_____

_____

_____

_____

(developed by Janis E. Mayer, Manchester Township Public Schools, Lakehurst, NJ) erable opportunity to interact with the general school population and have relatively easy access to a wide variety of student related data. Thus, the principal could easily gather information regarding student attendance and evidence of disruptive behaviors; the school nurse would have knowledge of a child's physical well-being and evidence of unnecessary absenteeism and nurse's office visits; the guidance counselor would have specific knowledge related to academic achievement, emotional well-being and other valuable information that may be collected from a student's permanent record file. Finally, concerned teachers would have, or be able to retrieve specific information regarding a student's in-class behavior and a child's circle of friends.

It is only through the team discussions that follow this systematic collection of student related data that strategies for remediation can begin. The flowchart on the following page illustrates the typical flow of information used to guide discussion regarding school intervention.

It is important to note that certain decisions are clearly guided by school policy or state law. For example, if the team concludes that a student is under the influence of a drug or alcohol, then specific school policy should be enacted and implemented so that the appropriate diagnostic, disciplinary and aftercare procedures can be put into effect. Similarly, conclusions related to child abuse and neglect must be reported to the appropriate social service agency (many states provide penalties for school personnel who fail to report suspected child abuse or neglect). In either case, the school must provide appropriate aftercare for students involved in the types of situations described above.

Parental Involvement

Once a child has been identified by the Student Assistance Team as being at significant risk it is absolutely essential that the child's parents play an active, supportive role in remediation. Data collected by the team should be presented to the parents in a non-threatening way. Parents should be urged to respond to their feelings, as well as to the accuracy of the data collected. Finally, the team should be prepared to address the student needs with an intervention plan which includes both school and home related activities.

In general, attempts at remediating the high-risk student will only be successful if parents are both supportive of the school's efforts and willing to assume the responsibility for direct involvement at home.

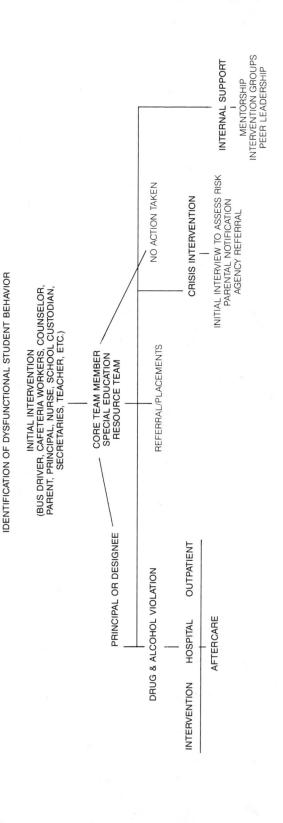

IDENTIFICATION OF DYSFUNCTIONAL STUDENT BEHAVIOR

INITIAL INTERVENTION
(BUS DRIVER, CAFETERIA WORKERS, COUNSELOR,
PARENT, PRINCIPAL, NURSE, SCHOOL CUSTODIAN,
SECRETARIES, TEACHER, ETC.)

CORE TEAM MEMBER
SPECIAL EDUCATION
RESOURCE TEAM

PRINCIPAL OR DESIGNEE

REFERRAL/PLACEMENTS

NO ACTION TAKEN

CRISIS INTERVENTION

INITIAL INTERVIEW TO ASSESS RISK
PARENTAL NOTIFICATION
AGENCY REFERRAL

INTERNAL SUPPORT

MENTORSHIP
INTERVENTION GROUPS
PEER LEADERSHIP

DRUG & ALCOHOL VIOLATION

INTERVENTION   HOSPITAL   OUTPATIENT

AFTERCARE

INTERVENTION STRATEGIES

Mentorships

For years intermediate level schools have had success with a variety of advisorship programs. Typically, a teaching staff member is assigned to 10–15 students to provide ongoing logistical and social support. Activities normally take place 2–3 times a week and provide the basis for healthy interchange between and among teachers and students. For most students of intermediate school age, this type of program can help with a wide variety of student centered concerns. Yet, those students who have been identified as disaffected of having the potential for destructive behaviors need the influence of a concerned adult each school day.

Thus, selected members of the school staff should serve as "mentors" to high-risk students. These mentors should be available both before and after each school day to 1–2 students. In general, the mentor would serve as an advocate for the high-risk child, providing a means of both monitoring and guiding his/her student through each school day.

How it Works—A Case Study
Mentorship

The following case study describes the role of a mentor in his dealings with an identified disaffected student:

Initial Referral

Joe, a seventh grade student, is referred to the Student Assistance Team by several teachers because of his inability to complete assignments, his alienation toward school, his chronic absenteeism, and his failure to make or keep friends.

Upon the analysis of all the data collected by the team, it is concluded that Joe is an intelligent individual who, given the appropriate guidance and taught the appropriate social skills, could, in fact, have a successful school experience.

Data Collection

To help analyze the nature of the situation, the team members are assigned the task of collecting pertinent information regarding Joe's academic, physical and emotional status. The team then reviews all available data and interviews several of Joe's teachers.

Parent Contact

A conclusion is reached that Joe would, in fact, benefit from the intervention of the Student Assistance Team. Joe's parents are contacted by the school's guidance counselor and invited to a team meeting. At this meeting, team members present a clear statement as to the nature of Joe's behavior in school, provide data to support their position and offer a school mentorship as a means to monitor and guide Joe's school activities. It is important that parents have the opportunity to share their perceptions of Joe's attitudes and behaviors so that a common assessment of need and a shared responsibility is developed.

Joe's parents agree to the assessment and give their support to the team intervention.

Initial Contact with Student

Mr. Nelson has volunteered (or can be assigned) as Joe's mentor. This team member has assumed his role because of his pre-established rapport with Joe and his interest in the mentorship program.

Mr. Nelson plans a meeting with Joe during a study hall period. Mr. Nelson describes the nature of the intervention and asks for Joe's cooperation in making the mentorship work. (Typically, students will be somewhat suspicious, yet, they are most often willing to try.)

Mr. Nelson explains to Joe that the primary responsibility for Joe's success in school will remain with Joe. Yet, he (Mr. Nelson) will meet with Joe every day before school to help organize him for the school day, discuss any problems that may have occurred outside of school, and deal with any issues that might prevent Joe from having a successful school day. Further, Joe is told that he (Mr. Nelson) will be available at the end of the school day to review what has happened to Joe during the day, organize homework assignments, help plan after-school priorities and time-lines, and, of course, be willing to listen and help Joe in any way that falls within the scope of his advocacy.

Other Planned Activities

Throughout the week, Mr. Nelson will monitor Joe's progress by speaking to his teachers; call Joe's parents to inform them of Joe's progress and to maintain parental support; develop a reward system for Joe so that positive reinforcement can be provided; and, particularly during school vacations or periods of absence from school, call and/or write Joe so that a genuine sense of caring is conveyed to Joe.

Administrative Support

It is important that "mentors" be given appropriate time to carry out their duties. Thus, these staff members should be relieved from homeroom, study hall, cafeteria and other non-instructional activities. Further, school funds should be made available to support the purchasing of notebooks, note pads, etc., to help organize students; to supply teachers with greeting cards and/or note paper to help maintain communication with students/parents; and to support established reward systems. It will be quite obvious that the gain in a student's academic achievement and self-esteem will more than justify the monetary and personnel expenditure.

Recordkeeping and Team Maintenance

It is important that a log be kept, describing the activities between the student and the mentor. This record should include the student's reactions toward the program, the student's progress (or lack of progress), and communications with parents, teachers or other involved adults.

It is important that the mentor shares his/her perceptions of the progress of the mentor relationship with other team members during regularly scheduled Student Assistance Team meetings. Through ongoing discussions, mentors can share strategies that have proved successful, share their frustrations, and gain the social support needed to maintain an enthusiastic commitment toward the program.

Experience with mentorship programs has provided a direct link with students who would normally be permitted to move through the school's grade levels without clear focus or sense of purpose. A mentor relationship can provide a student with the needed support to make schooling a more meaningful experience.

Intervention Groups

As the Student Assistance Team reviews the results of initial screenings and/or examines teachers' referrals, the members often observe common themes of student alienation with school, academic problems, family related problems, etc.

Intervention groups, aimed at bringing together students with similar problems, may help students better understand the nature of their dysfunctional feelings and behaviors and provide a basis for social support among students. Of course, parents must be notified of the goals and planned activities of the group.

Most importantly, these groups should be led by trained guidance counselors and/or professional staff members specifically trained in group dynamics and group facilitating.

Students Teaching Other Students

Older students in a school are a unique resource. They are near the age of their schoolmates and provide more realistic models for younger children than do adults who may seem so "far away" in years and attitudes.

Lippett (1975) provides several reasons for the popularity of programs where older students help younger ones. The programs provide:

— a mechanism to provide individualized instruction
— a means to promote friendships
— an avenue for increased motivation
— a method for older children to fill gaps in their learning
— a mechanism to launch communication and gain an appreciation between the ages
— a vehicle for students to learn competitive social skills

Schools have a ready supply of bright, eager students who have the potential of becoming positive role models for younger children. It is important, however, that schools take special care in the recruitment, selection and scheduling of peer tutors. Further, before a tutoring program is initiated, it is important that tutors are appropriately trained, are actively supervised, and are given specific direction to help ensure student mastery of skills.

The components of successful peer tutoring programs are characterized by:

— a highly structured and carefully prescribed lesson format
— specifically defined objectives related to a particular classroom curriculum
— selected tutoring content which is taught every day until a student learns it
— careful consideration of the frequency and duration of tutoring lessons
— ongoing, systematic tutor training
— daily measurement of students' progress

(Jenkins and Jenkins, 1987).

Peer tutoring can provide a more caring climate in the school, foster feelings of self-worth, improve academic proficiency, and maintain a positive linkage with students who may otherwise become alienated from school life.

CHILD ABUSE AND NEGLECT

Approximately twenty-five of every one thousand children are the subject of repeated maltreatment. It is estimated that as many as three times that number are actually victims of abuse (American Association for Protecting Children 1983 reports). These alarming figures place a significant number of students in every school population at high risk since incidence of child abuse and neglect clearly impact on a student's ability to learn.

Although reported cases of child abuse are in evidence at most every grade level, it is of particular importance for teachers in the middle grades to be aware of the increasing risks of sexual abuse cases for children between 10–13 years of age (AAPC, 1985). From a practical standpoint, school personnel see children on a daily basis and thus, offer a continuum of time to observe children. Further, school personnel are apt to notice changes in a child's behavior and temperament long before physical injury is detected.

The causes of child abuse are extremely complex, and this places certain limits on the school's overall impact on the problem. Yet, the schools have a role in: (1) making sure its personnel are not child abusers; (2) training its personnel to understand the nature of child abuse; (3) training its personnel to identify indicators of child abuse and neglect; and (4) providing opportunities in the curriculum for special programs that deal with the prevention and reporting of child abuse situations.

Types of Child Abuse

Essentially, there are four types of reported abuse (National Center on Child Abuse and Neglect, 1984):

1. Physical Abuse: Includes violent assault with an implement such as a knife or strap, burns, fractures, or other actions leading to possible injury to the child. "Spanking" for purely disciplinary reasons generally is not seen as child abuse.
2. Neglect: Physical—includes abandonment; refusal to seek,

allow or provide treatment for illness or impairment; inadequate physical supervision; disregard of health hazards in the home; and inadequate nutrition, clothing or hygiene when services are available.

Educational—includes knowingly permitting chronic truancy, keeping the child home from school repeatedly without cause, or failing to enroll a child in school.

3. Emotional Abuse: Includes verbal or emotional assault; close confinement such as tying or locking in closet; inadequate nurturance such as that affecting failure-to-thrive babies; knowingly permitting antisocial behavior such as delinquency, or serious alcohol/drug abuse; or refusal to allow medical care for a diagnosed emotional problem.

4. Sexual Abuse: Includes sexual molestation, incest, and exploitation for prostitution or the production of pornographic materials.

Legally, a "child" usually means a person under age 18. Child abuse and neglect occur at all stages of childhood, including adolescence (source: *Everything You Always Wanted to Know About Child Abuse and Neglect*, National Center on Child Abuse and Neglect, 1984).

As school personnel become increasingly aware of the nature of child abuse, it becomes the responsibility of school administration to develop strategies to help teachers identify those students who may be victims of abuse. The information provided below can serve as a benchmark for such training:

Symptoms of Child Abuse or Neglect

Type	Physical Indicators	Behavioral Indicators
Physical Abuse	Unexplained bruises and welts: • on face, lips, mouth • on torso, back, buttocks, thighs • in various stages of healing • clustered, forming regular patterns • reflecting shape of article used to inflict (electric cord, belt buckle)	Wary of adult contacts Apprehensive when other children cry Behavioral extremes • aggressiveness, or • withdrawal Frightened of parents Afraid to go home Reports injury by parents

(continued)

Symptoms of Child Abuse or Neglect *(continued)*

Type	Physical Indicators	Behavioral Indicators
Physical Abuse (continued)	• on several different surface areas • regularly appear after absence, weekend or vacation Unexplained burns: • cigar, cigarette burns, especially on soles, palms, back or buttocks • immersion burns (sock-like, glove-like, doughnut shaped on buttocks or genitalia) • patterned like electric burner, iron, etc. • rope burns on arms, legs, neck or torso Unexplained fractures: • to skull, nose, facial structure • in various stages of healing • multiple or spiral fractures Unexplained lacerations or abrasions: • to mouth, lips, gums, eyes • to external genitalia	
Physical Neglect	Consistent hunger, poor hygiene, inappropriate dress Consistent lack of supervision, especially in dangerous activities or long periods Unattended physical problems or medical needs Abandonment	Begging, stealing food Extended stays at school (early arrival and late departure) Constant fatigue, listlessness or falling asleep in class Alcohol or drug abuse Delinquency (e.g., thefts) States there is no caretaker
Sexual Abuse	Difficulty in walking or sitting Torn, stained or bloody underclothing Pain or itching in genital area Bruises or bleeding in external genitalia, vaginal or anal areas	Unwilling to change for gym or participate in physical education class Withdrawal, fantasy or infantile behavior Bizarre, sophisticated, or unusual sexual behavior or knowledge Poor peer relationships

(continued)

Symptoms of Child Abuse or Neglect *(continued)*

Type	Physical Indicators	Behavioral Indicators
Sexual Abuse (continued)	Venereal disease, especially in pre-teens Pregnancy	Delinquent or run away Reports sexual assault by caretaker
Emotional Maltreatment	Speech disorders Lags in physical development Failure-to-thrive	Habit disorders (sucking, biting, rocking, etc.) Conduct disorders (antisocial, destructive, etc.) Neurotic traits (sleep disorders, inhibition of play) Psychoneurotic reactions (hysteria, obsession, compulsion, phobias, hypochondria) Behavioral extremes: • compliant, passive • aggressive, demanding Overly adaptive behavior • inappropriately adult • inappropriately infant Developmental lags (mental, emotional) Attempted suicide

Source: The Educator's Role In The Prevention and Treatment of Child Abuse and Neglect, U.S. Department of Health and Human Services, 1984.

Finally, school personnel must be told that every state has a law mandating the reporting of suspected child abuse cases to the appropriate authorities. Further, in some states, educators can be fined or even imprisoned for failing to report.

While reporting is a general requirement, the procedures for reporting differ from state to state, and in many cases from school district to school district (see Kelley, *The Child Abuse Crisis,* 1985 for state-by-state reporting procedures). It is imperative that specific procedures, consistent with state law, are developed by each school district.

THE GIFTED ADOLESCENT GIRL

The number of gifted females appears to decline with age. By junior high school there are clearly more boys identified as gifted

$\top$ $\vdash$

than there are girls identified (Silverman, 1986). Despite early developmental advantages over boys (Hoffman, 1972) and no recognizable sex differences related to intellectual performance (Hyde, 1981), adolescence does, in fact, impact on female academic recognition. Although the situation is real, its causes are exceedingly complex. There is no evidence that girls lose ability as they mature. However, societal expectations and peer pressure to conform play a significant role in discouraging adolescent girls from competing academically with boys (see Maker, 1986 for an analysis of the critical issues in gifted education). Schools must become increasingly aware of this phenomenon and develop activities to better meet the needs of gifted adolescent females.

These activities may include:

— intervention groups for identified gifted adolescent girls

— special clubs for girls with high aptitude in math or science

— opportunities for gifted girls to visit with successful female professionals

— cluster scheduling of gifted girls in more academic areas to maintain a strong support network

PARENT INITIATIVES AND STUDENT ASSISTANCE

Without question, parents are a valuable source of information regarding their child's well-being. Parents should be encouraged to consider themselves as an active referral source for the Student Assistance Team. All too often parents are aware of children's patterns of unacceptable behavior but are often unable to determine their significance or are unwilling to involve the school in what they consider a "family concern." Frequently, parents must be educated as to the nature of high-risk behaviors. Workshops especially developed for parents in the identification of drug related paraphernalia and drug/alcohol related behaviors are of critical importance. Further, various parenting sessions to help meet the demands of dealing with adolescent children are advisable.

It is important that we not neglect the needs of parents during this critical time of their child's adolescence. As we plan programs and curriculum for staff and students, we must also encourage school leaders to provide meaningful opportunities for parents to more closely identify with the goals of our schools.

COMMUNITY AND SOCIAL SERVICE NETWORKING

It is very important that schools develop linkages with those community resources that can provide information, support and services to at-risk students. Schools should have an active listing of all local agencies that individually or collectively help provide an avenue for intervention for at-risk students and their families.

There are both legal and common sense limits to what schools can and should do in dealing with at-risk youngsters. School personnel must learn these limits and be able to refer the parents of the intermediate school age children to the appropriate resource.

SUMMARY

In this chapter, strategies for the identification and remediation of middle/junior high school students were explored. Additionally, strategies were developed specifically to address the dynamic characteristics of the early adolescent. Thus, although the general nature of effective schools can and should be used to guide school practices in the middle grades, it becomes increasingly important to tailor student assistance activities with those risk behaviors associated with the early adolescent child.

CHAPTER 5

Managing Risks to
Maximize Learning: Grades 9–12

There appears to be an inverse relationship between grade level and a perceived need for a focus on school/class climate. Clearly, and with reasonable justification, high schools typically are structured to promote academic initiatives and provide a program that prepares students for the academic challenge of college or the vocational challenges of the marketplace. However, while climate considerations are important during the early grades, it is somewhat paradoxical that it is these younger children who are typically intrinsically motivated and most easily influenced by adults. Essentially, these youngsters come to school with a "packaged positive climate."

Unfortunately, the complexities associated with growing up negatively impact on this intrinsic positive attitude of students and all too often reduce the likelihood of maximum learning. One must first acknowledge that attention to the rudiments of the research on effective schools and teachers does, in fact, play a significant role in the potential learning of all students regardless of grade. Climate of classrooms and schools will have a major impact on how students identify with their school as being a place where they want to be and want to learn.

Recognition of the importance of climate in high schools does not in any way reduce the focus on academic learning. One can safely argue that as obstacles and risks to learning are reduced, individual levels of academic achievement will increase.

This chapter will address the general nature of school culture, programs, and curricula as they relate to the well-being of high school students. Further, because of the significant nature of high-risk issues facing today's high school students and staff, specific chapters have been devoted to procedures, policy and programs related to selected critical issues. Thus, the topics of substance abuse, suicide, AIDS, eating disorders and teen pregnancy will be addressed in detail.

Finally, it is hoped that these final sections of the book will be used as a desk reference for school staff when confronted with the identified critical issues. As a practical framework the chapters that follow will provide specific prevention, intervention and after-care strategies. Additionally, sample policies, legal references, correspondence, memos, agendas, etc., are included as a relevant, time-saving mechanism to help frame an efficient response to very difficult situations.

ESTABLISHING AND REINFORCING POSITIVE NORMS

High school students are in a semi-adult place in life. They are still dependent on the home for support; and the school continues to provide a structured environment, with expectations for learning and behavior. However, many students enter part-time into the world of work, experience the freedom of being able to drive, go places on their own and date. With the new freedoms also come opportunities to make really serious mistakes, such as becoming teen parents, depending on drugs, being involved in car accidents and/or dropping out of school.

A school staff which has high expectations for students is essential for the development of a positive school climate. In addition, clear parameters for student behavior have to be set and enforced. Expectations for staff must include the establishment of a positive learning climate in the classroom, as well as the teaching of subject matter content. The staff, led by the principal, needs to develop a school atmosphere conducive to learning. Personnel must help minimize risks and be ready to assist students who experience problems.

High school students are heavily influenced both positively and negatively by their peers. An advantage of working with high school age students is that they are sophisticated enough to assist each other in avoiding problems and in addressing difficulties when they occur. Peer support programs can be developed to help prevent some of the negative responses to predictable problems of students and to reinforce positive norms in the school. Peer support programs can range from relatively informal arrangements such as assigning senior volunteers to meet with one or more incoming freshmen for discussion of high school rules and activities, to regularly scheduled group sessions using trained student leaders and a standardized curriculum. Following are some examples of peer support programs.

Senior/Freshmen Orientation Program

The purpose of many peer support programs is to ease the transition of younger students into the high school environment. Freshmen are frequently confused and apprehensive about high school. Volunteer seniors or juniors with some training can assist in helping students make the transition. There are also benefits for the peer counselors. The opportunity to assume a leadership role, think through the problems of others, serve as a role model, and actually help someone else, frequently has a more positive effect on the leader than the students being assisted. A peer support program also brings freshmen into contact with students who are positive role models and may reduce the chances for students to be influenced by those students who would be negative models. Finally, a freshmen support program can help the school break up what may be an informal hazing system and replace it with a program supportive of freshmen.

How it Works—A Case Study
Senior/Freshmen Orientation

The senior class advisor, senior class president, two junior students, guidance counselor and a student assistance team member plan the Freshmen Orientation Program in the spring. The students interview a number of freshmen, from varying groups within the school, to determine what their concerns were and what problems they encountered when they came to the high school. The student information is combined with general information which all freshmen will need.

An eighth grade orientation is planned. The guidance counselor presents an overview of the high school program and the steps the incoming freshmen will need to take to schedule classes. A junior student explains that in the fall each freshmen will be assigned a senior guide. The guide will help answer questions about the school and program. Following the formal presentation the eighth graders meet in groups of 8–10 with a male and female junior student to ask questions about the high school. Junior volunteers will have met with the guidance counselor prior to the session to discuss typical concerns and to role-play a meeting.

A job description for a senior guide or leader is developed. It includes required contacts with freshmen assigned in groups and individually; description of the role of senior guide; procedures to follow if serious problems are brought to the senior guide. The junior class officers ask juniors for volunteers to serve as freshmen guides in the fall of their senior year. After the volunteers are screened and selected, an orientation session is held in the spring and tentative lists of three to six incoming freshmen are given to each guide. On the first day of school in the fall, a second orientation meeting is held and new students are added to lists and students who have moved are dropped. The counselor and the senior advisor are available to the student guides if problems arise. The program is implemented from September through December.

Peer Counseling Groups

A full-scale Peer Counseling Group program requires Board, administration and staff leadership commitment. Planning, training and financial resources are required. Models and training programs can be found around the country. Models vary in terms of training needed and the roles played by students; however, they tend to have some elements in common, including a process for selecting students to be peer leaders; a course or summer training program for peer leaders; a staff member who manages the program, provides the training and who has a reduced load of classes; additional staff members who work with the program; a scheduled set of small group sessions for freshmen on specific topics run by two peer leaders (male and female); a written curriculum; supervision of the group sessions by a trained faculty member; opportunities for the peer leaders to meet frequently to discuss the program and problems; and planned communication program with parents and other staff. While peer group leadership programs require a major investment of commitment, time and resources, they can be effective for both the freshmen in the groups and for the peer leaders.

Peer Tutoring

A review of data associated with school dropouts, chronic discipline cases, drug and alcohol abuse, teenage pregnancy, depression, and vandalism makes it apparent that school failure or low grades are often listed among the underlying causes. It makes common sense that if a student is not meeting success in his/her academic classes that he/she will feel a sense of failure and seek other areas which will allow him/her to "escape" or gain other types of recognition. Helping students to succeed in school is an obvious means for assisting students, with peer tutoring being an effective means for supplementing other forms of academic assistance. The effectiveness of the approach has been validated in programs across the country and with varying age groups.

Some interesting things have been found about peer tutoring or peer teaching. First, tutors have to want to be tutors, but they do not have to be the top students to be effective. Frequently a student who has had trouble with a subject will be more sympathetic towards another student who has the same problem and will be better able to explain the subject. Second, the tutors gain as much or more from the program than the person tutored in terms of increased self-esteem and in understanding of the subject. Also, the student being tutored learns the subject matter and is better prepared to succeed academically (Highland Park School District, 1980).

As with any other program, planning is necessary. The tutors need to be guided in their role: there must be a method of identifying tutors, matching tutors to students needing tutoring and the opportunity for tutors and students to meet. In some cases a school-wide program might be planned; in other cases a department might arrange for tutoring in subjects taught by that department only. The Student Assistance Team might directly plan and implement a tutoring program. In the beginning a small group of tutors might be used to assist students who are returning from extended absences.

Teen Planning Groups

The strategies used by a school to prevent major student problems or to assist students in coping with problems must be matched to the problems, needs and backgrounds of the students in the school. For example, in some schools alcohol may be a major problem but not pills, marijuana or heroin. A scare film on heroin shown to the kids may appear to them irrelevant and reinforce the feeling that the adults in the school don't know what is going on with kids. A way of targeting programs to meet the needs of students is to get them involved in planning prevention and assistance activities.

Such a planning group needs to be led by a faculty member who: has good rapport with a wide variety of students; has at least some knowledge of prevention, assistance strategies and resources; and has the confidence of the school administration. Not all suggestions made by the teenagers will be workable or appropriate. However, students may be able to help implement in a better manner some programs already planned or in operation. The message they recommend may be the same as that of the faculty planners, but students may have a better sense of how to deliver the message effectively to the specific student body in that school. Students in the planning group need to be from all sub-peer cultures in the school, not just the "good" students. Strategies have to have an effect on the unmotivated students, the students with overt problems, the jocks, the working students, the withdrawn students as well as the popular class leaders.

Some of the activities which students might plan and implement are:

— Development of videos showing how peer pressure is used in the school to get kids to drink or use other drugs, how to resist the pressure or how rumors are spread throughout the school

— Planning and giving non-drink and non-drug parties which illustrate you can have fun without drinking

— Holding meetings with parents at which students role-play problems, followed by small group discussions with parents and students

— Holding group discussion sessions with peers to talk about pressures

— Planning assembly programs which are targeted to problems in that particular school

CURRICULUM TO REDUCE RISK, GRADES 9-12

Schools can assist students to reduce risks to learning through direct instruction. The high school curriculum should build on the curriculum of the lower grades. Knowledge concerning drugs/alcohol, pregnancy, venereal disease (including AIDS) should continue to be presented. Although most of the general "facts" will already be known to the students from health and science study in the earlier grades, the factual information needs to be linked to both the positive and negative consequences of actions. For example, students need to know more than facts about use. They need to learn parenting skills and the responsibilities involved in parenting. They also need to know the physical, social and psychological risks of teenage pregnancy: both to the mother and the baby. They need to understand the life skills involved in being an adult and the life skills needed by a teenager to resist negative peer and adult pressures.

In most high schools the major responsibility for teaching life skills is part of the health curriculum. However, topics related to the health and adjustment of students do not need to be limited to the formal health curriculum. Science, social studies, career education classes and English classes also provide opportunities to strengthen student life skills.

STUDENT ASSISTANCE PROGRAM, GRADES 9–12

There are many high-school-level areas in which students require assistance. They include:

— academic counseling and course selection
— career counseling
— college selection and admissions assistance
— referral and appropriate placement if a handicapping condition exists
— remediation assistance in academic areas
— an academically challenging program for the bored
— sports and extracurricular outlets

Unfortunately, there are other areas where teens may require assistance—areas in which the student may not seek help or may even resist getting help. These include:

— drug and alcohol abuse
— suicidal thoughts or behavior
— pregnancy
— venereal disease
— child abuse
— chronic discipline problems
— absentee problems
— eating disorders

Most schools are fairly well set up to handle the first set of student needs. Guidance counselors, while frequently serving far too many students, attend to academic, career and college placements. The special education staff addresses the needs of those meeting the criteria for special education. State, federal, and local programs provide supplemental support, in at least the basic skills, for students below academic standards. Advance placement and honors courses may be available for the academically gifted. A wide variety of sports and extracurricular activities are supported by most schools. Counselors try, along with their other duties, to counsel individual students who want their help.

What about the second set of problems faced by students? Problems which at the least limit student learning and in the extreme damage or destroy a young person's life. The effects of these serious problems spread beyond the individual since they negatively affect other students and the instructional climate of the classroom. Teachers complain that they don't know what to do about the student who falls asleep in class, seems disengaged, is aggressive, indifferent or exhibits a host of other negative behaviors. They complain that they report the problem to the administration but nothing much is done. In serious behavior cases the student may get detention or even be suspended, but then he/she is back in class and the general pattern of behavior may continue.

A Student Assistance Program is designed to help the school work effectively with problems arising from: drug and alcohol abuse, suicidal behavior, pregnancy, venereal disease, child abuse, weight problems, chronic discipline problems, and absenteeism. The program is based on the following premises:

- that it is a legitimate role of the school to intervene in situations which limit the learning and potential of students
- that the school staff working in a coordinated and planned manner can enhance the learning environment for individual students and the student body at large
- that the school has the obligation to work with parents to get help for students
- that a Student Assistance Program does not supplant other services available in the school but ensures that there is an avenue of assistance for all students
- that a Student Assistance Program provides assistance not therapy
- that Student Assistance Program activities should be conducted by a team and not be delegated to an individual
- that a Student Assistance Program must be sanctioned by the Board and actively supported by the administration
- that a Student Assistance Program will not solve every problem, nor will it prevent all crises
- that there is no such thing as confidentiality when a student is in danger
- that the staff has an obligation to intervene in situations

potentially dangerous to the student with or without the student's permission

A Student Assistance Program can include one or more of the following: aftercare support groups, problem solving groups, inhouse suspension, peer counseling, life skills classes, parent and student information programs, and community and school cooperative programs.

The Student Assistance Team

The Student Assistance Team (or Crisis Team or Student Support Team) is composed of volunteer staff members who are trained to identify either students-at-risk or any school situations which are risks to students and to intervene with the students or in risk situations.

The usual configuration of a team includes a school administrator, school nurse, two or three teachers and a counselor. It is essential that an administrator be part of the team, in order to interpret school rules and to provide support to the rest of the staff. Since many of the problems faced by the team have health implications the school nurse is also an important member. Teachers should be selected from volunteers and should be familiar with various types of students, be committed to getting help for troubled students, be able to work effectively as members of a team, and be able to accept that they will not always be in a position to assist all students. Large schools may require more than one team.

There are also some staff members who should not be considered for the team. These include the amateur therapists—the teachers who pride themselves on working alone with students to solve their problems; teachers who brag that students confide their drug/alcohol use to them and how they are "helping" these students to kick the habit. In cases of drug/alcohol dependency or suicidal depression even the most skilled professionals, using the most intense treatment programs, have only moderate success rates with adolescents. The staff member who thinks he/she alone can "save" the child is deluding him-/herself and will not contribute to the team's effort to get the child qualified help.

Employing a Crisis or Student Assistance Counselor

A number of schools are hiring a drug/alcohol counselor usually under the title of Student Assistance Counselor or Crisis Counselor. The training of these individuals may be limited to drug and alcohol problems or be broad based. Such individuals can provide valuable assistance in:

- identifying students with problems
- interviewing students concerning changes in behavior
- serving as an obvious and available source of assistance for students experiencing problems
- working with the Student Assistance Team
- working with other counselors
- working with parents and outside agencies
- arranging and conducting after-support programs

The student assistance counselor should not be hired to be "the" Student Assistance Program. As in the case of individual guidance counselors, child study team members or teachers cannot meet all the needs of students; one person designated as a student assistance counselor cannot possibly handle the number of student problems encountered in a typical high school.

The role of the student assistance counselor needs to be carefully defined in relationship to other professionals in the school and to the total Student Assistance Program. Once defined and developed, the role needs to be communicated effectively to students, staff, parents and board of education members.

The Role of the Student Assistance Team

The mission of the school is learning. The goal of the Student Assistance Team is to identify behaviors which are impeding the learning of students and to get them the help needed so they can become productive learners and members of the school community. To accomplish this goal, the team conducts the following activities:

- accepts referrals from teachers, administrators, parents and students
- gathers information concerning the reported problem
- discusses the information and decides on a course of action
- provides feedback to the referring teacher
- refers the student to another person or group within the school
- refers the student to out-of-school assistance
- discusses the problem with the parents and student
- confronts the parent and student with the situation when necessary
- monitors the student's behavior
- arranges for after-support for the student

Scheduling the Activities of the Student Assistance Team

The activities of the Student Assistance Team are time-consuming, emotionally difficult activities as well as emotionally rewarding, and are likely to lead to initial criticism from parents of children identified as having potentially serious problems. There has to be commitment on the part of the Board of Education, central administration and the school administration to support a Student Assistance Program and a Student Assistance Team.

Responsibilities as a member of the Student Assistance Team cannot be added onto a complete load of classes and other responsibilities. Nor can the administration expect teachers to give up planning periods on a regular basis. Functioning after the school day has two drawbacks. First, the staff is tired and secondly, other teachers with whom the team needs to communicate have left for the day. During the planning stages, temporary arrangements may be acceptable. However, once the program becomes operational, stable arrangements need to be made

Probably the easiest and least expensive way to provide time for the Student Assistance Team to function is to schedule all team members to be available for the same non-teaching duty period. Instead of being assigned to study hall duty or cafeteria duty the team members are assigned student assistance. During the course of a week the team might meet formally two or three times and use the other two or three periods to collect data and meet with students or parents. In addition, there may be times when the team will have to meet with parents after school hours, or depending on the program, run support groups after school. This additional time might be volunteer time, be recognized by a stipend such as that paid for coaching or by elimination of other school duties such as homeroom.

If adequate provision is not made for the team, even the most enthusiastic group will quickly "burn out." Burnout can also be a problem for the chairperson of the team. It is recommended that chairmanship of the team be rotated so that one person doesn't always have the burden.

Training the Student Assistance Team

The Student Assistance Team must be trained to conduct the specific activities of the program. Ideally the training will be provided by a person experienced in training teams. Some state departments of education are equipped to provide the training. In

other cases members of functioning teams from other schools may
be utilized. The team does not have to be taught all at once how to
handle all problems. For example, training may start with a focus
on handling the most common problem, drug and alcohol abuse.
Following implementation of a program in that area, training in
suicide prevention may begin. However, the initial training must
include:

— purpose of the team
— team development
— knowledge of the problems, means and reasons for collecting
   information
— documenting the case
— student interview techniques
— techniques for working with parents
— techniques for confronting parents and students
— how to work with agencies
— strategies for follow-up support
— how to work as a team
— strategies for maintaining the team over time
— essentials of a team plan

The training will take four to five days. Additional training will
be needed for those who will run group sessions.

Defining the Relationship Between the
Student Assistance Team and other Groups and Individuals

The Student Assistance Team is complementary to other student
services groups within the school and district; however, it is essential that the roles of the various groups be defined and the relationships be determined. Some of the groups and individuals whose
roles must be included in the total plan are: the disciplinarian
(he/she may be a team member), guidance, the special education
staff, nurse, and school physician. Some of these individuals and
groups, such as the Child Study Team, may have legal constraints
on what they can and cannot do. However, most of the students
referred to the Student Assistance Team will not be classified students and even in cases where they are, Child Study Teams and
Student Assistance Teams can work in a cooperative fashion.
Individual members of the Child Study Team may also be in position to provide training and support to Student Assistance Team
members. The important thing is to think out the relationships

High School
Student Assistance Program Organization

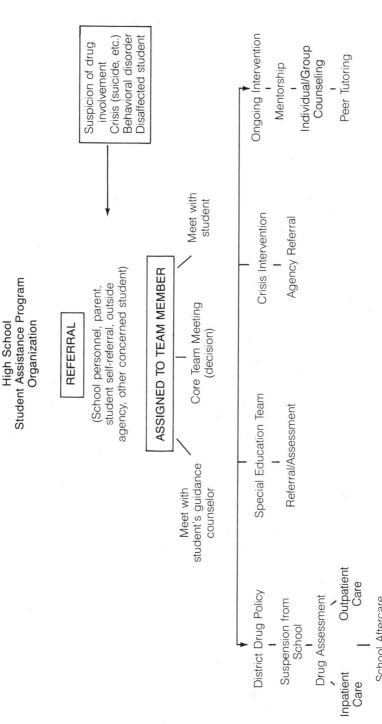

REFERRAL

(School personnel, parent, student self-referral, outside agency, other concerned student)

Suspicion of drug involvement
Crisis (suicide, etc.)
Behavioral disorder
Disaffected student

ASSIGNED TO TEAM MEMBER

Meet with student's guidance counselor

Meet with student

Core Team Meeting (decision)

Special Education Team

Referral/Assessment

Crisis Intervention

Agency Referral

Ongoing Intervention
Mentorship
Individual/Group Counseling
Peer Tutoring

District Drug Policy
Suspension from School
Drug Assessment
Inpatient Care
Outpatient Care
School Aftercare

before problems arise and develop a flowchart of services. (See sample on page 77.)

How it Works—A Case Study
The Student Assistance Team in Action

Each situation which is brought to the attention of the Student Assistance Team is unique in some way; however, there is a general pattern which guides the team's actions. Following is an example of how a hypothetical case might be handled.

Monday Morning—Initial Referral

Mrs. Jones, an English teacher, stops Mr. Smith in the faculty room. Mrs. Jones has some concerns about Mary, a student in her class. Mary's grades have dropped and she seems disinterested in class. Mr. Smith asks Mrs. Jones to complete a referral form and promises to look into the situation (see sample form).

Tuesday Fifth Period—Team Meeting

Mr. Smith discusses the information on the referral form, completed by Mrs. Jones, with the team. They decide to gather a complete set of information since there is some reason for concern. All of Mary's teachers will be asked to complete referral forms; the nurse will complete a form concerning any visits. Mary's attendance record will be reviewed along with any disciplinary action. A team member will meet with her guidance counselor to find out if there are any reported or obvious problems (i.e., a very ill family member).

Friday Fifth Period—Team Meeting

The team discusses findings. Mary's grades have also dropped slightly in French, but none of the other teachers report any academic problems. Mary has been absent quite a bit, but always brings a note from home. No serious pattern of behavior appears evident. It is decided that a member of the team will meet with Mary.

Monday Fifth Period—Meeting with Mary

Mr. Smith meets with Mary and explains that some of her teachers are concerned about her. Their concern is that in two classes her grades have dropped and she seems disinterested. He asks if there is a reason. Mary explains that her father lost his job and she is concerned that she will not be able to afford college. She is working almost 40 hours a week between her babysitting jobs and employment in a local store. After work she is frequently too tired to write essays for English or spend the hours required for some of her French homework. Mr. Smith suggests that Mary meet with her guidance counselor to discuss scholarship and loan programs. He also suggests that she limit her working to 20 hours a week. Mary agrees to see her counselor.

Tuesday Fifth Period—Team Meeting

Mr. Smith reports on the meeting with Mary. He has also spoken with her counselor and determined that Mary has made an appointment. He feels Mary will qualify for college aid as long as her grades do not drop. Mr. Smith will speak to the English and French teachers about what the team has determined. The team decides to send out another set of referral forms to Mary's teachers at the end of the marking period, to see if the situation has improved.

Fortunately, many referrals will involve relatively straightforward problems. The Student Assistance Team will be able to assist students to solve problems or guide them to others who can help. Examples of how the team can handle other more serious problems are provided in the sections dealing with those problems.

Student Assistance Team Referral & Information Request

Student _____ School _____

Grade _____ Date _____ Period(s) _____

Subject(s) _____

Other contact with student:

Coach _____ Guidance _____ Administrator _____ Other _____

Referred by: _____

Staff _____ Peer _____ Parent _____ Self _____

I. General Observations Concerning Student
   - ☐ Low academic performance
   - ☐ Poor attendance
   - ☐ Behavior problems
   - ☐ Discipline code violation
   - ☐ Physical problems
   - ☐ Change in behavior and/or performance
   - ☐ Personal problems
   - ☐ Other (briefly explain) _____

(continued)

☐ I have not observed any behaviors which are of concern
(if you check here you need not complete the rest of this form)

II. **Specific Observations: Please check all behaviors you have observed. In a few cases, dates and/or numbers are needed.**

A. **Academic performance**
☐ Grades have been consistent
☐ Grades have declined (on tests—for marking period _____ on assignments _____
☐ Work is incomplete or not submitted
☐ Unprepared for class
☐ Does not participate in class. Is this a change in behavior? _____
☐ Suspected or confirmed cheating
☐ Poor short-term memory for subject matter
☐ Rationalization for poor performance
☐ Placement in this class appears to be inappropriate based on the student's general ability _____, interests _____, background in the subject area _____
☐ Poor reading skills
☐ Short attention span; easily distracted
☐ Claims to be unable to remember assignments or other class responsibilities

B. **Attendance**
☐ Number of excused absences this school year _____
Dates of absences in the past 8 weeks: _____
☐ Number of times late to class _____
☐ Number of cuts: Dates _____
☐ On absence list but in school: Dates if known _____
☐ Frequent requests to leave class to go to:
Nurse _____ Guidance _____ Restroom _____ Locker _____
Other _____

C. **Behavior**
☐ Defiance of rules
☐ Lethargic
☐ Withdrawn
☐ Suspected or confirmed lying
☐ Obscene behavior or gestures
☐ Arguing with teachers
☐ Arguing with other students
☐ Attention-getting behavior
☐ Passing notes or materials to other students
☐ Unable to sit still for more than a few minutes
☐ Destruction of property
☐ Aggressive behavior
☐ Outburst of anger
☐ Excessive talking
☐ Inability to _____
☐ Crying
☐ Other

(continued)

D. **Physical Problems**
- ☐ Attempts to sleep in class
- ☐ Unkempt physical appearance
- ☐ This is a change which was noted approximately _____ weeks ago
- ☐ This is a periodic observation
- ☐ This has been the case since the student has been in my class
- ☐ Complaints of not feeling well (general)
- ☐ Frequent cold-like symptoms
- ☐ Requests to go to the nurse
- ☐ Smelling of alcohol or marijuana
- ☐ Poor physical ability
- ☐ There has been a decline in physical ability
- ☐ Reluctance to participate in physical activities
- ☐ Dropped from team:
  self-initiated _____ by coach _____
- ☐ Missed practices without substantive reason
- ☐ Unexplained injuries
- ☐ Slurred speech
- ☐ Frequent complaints of nausea or vomiting
- ☐ Unsteady on feet
- ☐ Weight loss
- ☐ Other

E. **Change in Behavior or Performance**
- ☐ Change of friends
- ☐ Friends raise concern about changes in behavior
- ☐ Erratic behavior
- ☐ Giving away personal possessions
- ☐ Friends who are older or younger
- ☐ Secretive behavior (i.e., requests to leave without telling why, passing notes)
- ☐ Seeking adult contact
- ☐ Talk about drugs/alcohol
- ☐ Talk about partying
- ☐ Change in personality
  - ☐ more aggressive
  - ☐ more withdrawn
  - ☐ other
- ☐ Changes in goals or future plans
- ☐ Sudden popularity
- ☐ Defensiveness
- ☐ Responses inappropriate to situation
- ☐ Complaints about school
- ☐ Loss of eligibility for sports and extracurricular activities
- ☐ Dropped out of extracurricular activity:
  Activity _____
  Approximate date of drop _____
- ☐ Missed activity meetings without substantive reason

(continued)

F. Discipline
    ☐ Suspended number of times _____
       Reason for suspension
       _____ Dates _____
       _____ Dates _____
       _____ Dates _____
       _____ Dates _____
    ☐ Retention number of times _____
       Reason for retention
       _____ Dates _____
       _____ Dates _____
       _____ Dates _____
       _____ Dates _____
    ☐ Student sent to the office for discipline: number of times _____
       Reason for sending
       _____ Dates _____
       _____ Dates _____
       _____ Dates _____
       _____ Dates _____
    ☐ Student required to stay after school with teacher:
       Reason for action
       _____
       _____
       _____
       _____

G. Home/Social/Family/Out-of-School Problems
    ☐ Complaints about personal problems
    ☐ Complaints of family problems
    ☐ Recent changes in family situation
       Illness _____ Death _____ Changed family structure _____
       Information is confidential _____
    ☐ Student works
       ☐ Recently obtained a job
       ☐ Changed jobs
       ☐ Increased hours
       ☐ Other
    ☐ Student quit job _____ or was fired _____
    ☐ Student observed outside of school with non-family adults
    ☐ Student observed outside of school with students who have
       dropped out _____ graduated _____
    ☐ Talks about partying
    ☐ Has run away from home in the past
    ☐ Avoids peers

Comments: Please provide any other information which may help the team understand the student's behavior.

Note: The information you provide will be reviewed along with information from other staff members. The information will not become part of the student's permanent file and general confidentiality will be maintained. If the team concludes that the student is experiencing serious problems, specific information may be shared with the student and his/her parents. Under the Board of Education policy, staff members are considered "save harmless" for providing information concerning behavior of students which may be harmful to the student.

CONFIDENTIALITY AND THE NEED TO KNOW

It has already been stated that in cases of danger or potential danger to the student there can be no confidentiality. However, what about non-dangerous situations? The team will have to balance respect for the privacy of the student against the need for others to know certain information if they are going to help.

In the example above, it would be appropriate for Mr. Smith to share the information concerning Mary with her counselor. He should also tell Mary he is going to do this. On the other hand, the teachers need to know that the situation was reviewed and some action taken, but they don't need to know all the details. Mr. Smith might share with the English teacher that Mary has been working long hours after school, but not that Mary's father lost his job. Other teachers may only need to know that the information they provided was reviewed and was helpful to the team. Mary should be made aware of what will be told to her teachers.

Under no circumstances should information discussed by or brought to the team become part of the general conversation in the teacher's room or be shared with others who have no need to know.

Records of the Student Assistance Team should be kept separate from other student records in a secure location. In some states certain information may be required to be added to the student's official file. The team should review laws concerning records and their own Board policies on the subject. In most situations parents will have a right to review the records.

TEAM MAINTENANCE

Teams typically begin their work enthusiastically. However, over time they can become tired of the extra work, frustrated by some failures, annoyed at other staff members and aggravated by other team members. For these and other reasons the team needs to schedule time to discuss the team and its interactions with each other and with those outside the team. These must be open and honest exchanges. Some typical problems which team members encounter are:

– feelings that they are doing a disproportionate part of the work

— that part of the team is a clique and excludes others on the team
— that one person is trying to run the show
— that their opinions are not valued

Discussion will not always solve the problems but at least it gets them on the table and raises the possibility of solutions before problems become critical. The agenda for the scheduled maintenance meeting should include: How are we doing as a team? How can we work more effectively as team? The team should agree in advance that the goal of these meetings will be improved team effectiveness. There is no room for "I gotcha" agendas. Failure to adequately attend to team maintenance is a major reason for failure of Student Assistance Teams.

SUMMARY

This chapter dealt with the need to focus on school/class climate at the secondary level. Strategies for developing and reinforcing positive norms were presented. Further, the role of curriculum in reducing risks to learning was discussed.

The development of a pro-active student assistance program was presented. Central to this approach was the definition of the role of the school in assisting students who are at risk, and the establishment, operation and maintainance of a Student Assistance Team. A case study illustrated how students are referred and how the program works.

CHAPTER 6

Drug and Alcohol Abuse—Prevention, Assistance, Confrontation, Aftercare

THE PROBLEM

Two-thirds of all teenagers will use drugs before they graduate from high school (University of Michigan, 1986).

About 40 percent of high school students use drugs other than alcohol or marijuana (University of Michigan, 1986).

While it may take adults years to become truly addicted to drugs/alcohol, teenagers can become addicted in less than six months (Horton, 1985).

Most teenage unwanted pregnancies began when one or both of the partners were under the influence of drugs/alcohol (Pennsylvania Department of Education, 1986).

Drugs/alcohol are involved in two out of three suicides (Bolton, 1986).

Drugs/alcohol use are major contributors to school failure and dropping out of school (United States Department of Education, 1986).

Drug/alcohol dependency is a major contributor to crimes such as stealing and violence (United States Department of Education, 1986).

Teachers, school administrators, guidance counselors, doctors, parents and other students often contribute to the development of drug/alcohol dependency by denial, well-meaning but ineffective assistance, ignorance, evading the situation or in the case of some psychiatrists, prescription of drugs.

Societal attitudes that there are "safe" or "soft" drugs such as alcohol and marijuana and "dangerous" drugs such as cocaine or speed, ignore the facts that all drugs are dangerous for minors.

Teenagers often act as if they believe they are immortal. "It can happen to Johnny but not to me."

Students who use drugs/alcohol have a spillover effect on other students. They pose the threat of involving other students in the use of drugs/alcohol. They also take a disproportionate part of the teacher's time in class.

Students from drug/alcohol dependent homes are more apt to become dependent and are more apt to experience other problems such as child abuse and eating disorders.

THE ROLE OF THE SCHOOL IN
DRUG/ALCOHOL PREVENTION AND ASSISTANCE

Schools alone cannot prevent drug and alcohol abuse or cure the abuse when it occurs. Substance abuse is a complex and long-term problem. A recent study by Sheppard Kellam (1987) found that antisocial first-graders were more likely than other students to be involved in drug abuse ten years later. Patterns of behavior and attitudes developed at a very early age may determine to a great degree the level of risk of addiction experienced by the student. Society at large also gives contradictory messages concerning the use of drugs and alcohol, particularly in the case of smoking and alcohol. Advertisements, media programs, and frequently, parents, associate the use of alcohol and cigarettes with a "good time." In the case of smoking the evidence of health risks is overwhelming. In the case of alcohol, there is little evidence that a drink or two will have long-term negative health effects on adults, except when combined with driving. Research consistently shows that some people are more genetically and environmentally at risk of becoming substance abusers than are others.

Another major problem is denial. Alcohol and drug addiction is a disease; however, it is not seen by the person involved as a problem. To a drug/alcohol dependent person the substance is his/her "best friend"—a friend to be protected at all costs. Mental health professionals frequently make the statement that "the only time a drug/alcohol dependent person is lying is when his/her lips are moving." In the early stages of drug/alcohol abuse, the person is conscious of his/her lies. In later stages the pattern of lying and rationalization becomes so dominant that he/she usually cannot differentiate truth from fiction. Dependent people will promise they will stop, deny they have a problem and use any available means to keep their addiction. Unfortunately, they are frequently helped to continue in denial by "enablers." These are other people who are usually well meaning but by their actions or lack of actions assist the dependent person to continue their habit. Parents frequently play this role. They do not recognize the signs of problems in their child's behavior, are afraid they will lose the child's love if they confront him/her, simply do not know what to do, or blame their child's behavior on the actions of themselves or others. Teachers can also be enablers by not knowing what behaviors are associated with risk, overlooking negative behaviors, trying to assist the student to "cure" him/herself, fear of reprisal if they take action, and fear that students will not like them if they take action. Schools as a whole can serve as enablers by denying that dependency problems exist, discouraging staff from taking action, not backing staff who intervene with students, and not establishing policies, intervention guidelines, curriculum and assistance programs.

While controlling student drug and alcohol use is difficult, schools can play a significant and positive role. Because the problem is complex, only a multifaceted program will be effective. Expectations for the program must recognize limitations, since no school program will prevent all substance abuse. The basic strategies available to the school are:

— effective teaching of decision-making skills, negative peer resistance skills, and facts concerning the dangers of drug/alcohol
— the setting of tough policies, guidelines and procedures which make it clear to students, staff and parents that drug/alcohol use will not be tolerated
— training staff to recognize and act upon signs of drug/alcohol use
— providing opportunities for students to seek help for themselves or others
— establishing a proactive plan and procedures for identifying students with problems and assisting them to get help
— developing a plan for working with parents as a group and with parents of individual students
— establishing procedures and plans for working with community groups
— establishing a procedure for confrontation, complete with penalties, to get help for students who resist assistance or whose parents resist assistance
— enforcing the penalties for drug/alcohol use or sale established by the school board and law
— establishing procedures for working with the police
— building strong working relationships with outside agencies which provide therapy and support programs for addicted students

- providing group and individual support for school related problems for students returning from treatment
- providing as much support as possible to all students so they will succeed academically and socially in the school environment

It is not the role of the school to provide therapy for students who are abusing drugs/alcohol or who are addicted. The addicted student is both physically and psychologically dependent. Drugs/alcohol are his "best friend." He/she is not going to give them up by confiding in a teacher his/her use or by saying he/she wants to give them up. There are very good reasons why even the best trained professionals in drug/alcohol addiction field, and the best developed programs have only limited success in treating adolescent drug/alcohol abusers. Drug/alcohol abuse is a disease that is exceedingly hard to treat, and recurrence of the disease is likely. Therefore, a teacher who attempts to "treat" the addicted student is deluding him- or herself and is increasing the risk to the child.

The school cannot ignore the problem of drug/alcohol use and abuse among students (or among staff members). The problem is there, it is a progressive disease, it will continue to be there, and it will get worse if it is ignored, thus affecting the ability of the school to complete its mission of educating students.

THE DRUG/ALCOHOL CURRICULUM

do NOT

T F

Most students know the facts about drugs and alcohol by the time they are in high school. The "facts" as students perceive them may consist of a mix of scientifically based information and myths gathered from the media and peers. Hopefully, students will have been taught accurate information on drugs and alcohol starting in the elementary grades. However, knowing the facts alone will not prevent or even significantly reduce student drug abuse. The high school curriculum, however, should include:

- information on assessing the student's own risk of addiction
- information on assessing the risk of other students and adults of addiction
- how "enabling" behaviors can be controlled
- the effect of substance abuse on the family, both physical and psychological
- strengthening of problem analysis and problem solving skills
- improving positive peer relationship skills

- identification of the effects of alcohol and drugs on the body and, during pregnancy, on the fetus
- effects of alcohol and drugs on driving
- treatment of alcohol and drug addiction
- how to get help for yourself or others

With the departmental structure of the typical high school the health course is the most likely place to develop and implement the drug and alcohol curriculum. Many states have drug and alcohol curriculum requirements and guidelines for curriculum development. "Here's Looking At You, 2000" (Seattle, Washington, 1986) is an outstanding program which provides the teacher with all the material and lessons needed for instruction (see sample checklist). Much time and resources can be saved by adoption of a well-designed and tested program rather than in developing a new program.

If driver education is taught as a separate course in the school, then the effects of drugs and alcohol on driving should be emphasized in the course. Driver simulation machines are now available which allow a student to "experience" the effects on driving under the influence of varying amounts of alcohol or drugs. Such simulations have potentially greater effect on student behavior than being lectured on the subject.

Scope and Sequence

"Here's Looking At You, 2000" presents drug-related issues in a comprehensive manner from kindergarten through twelfth grade. The curriculum was developed so that students could progress through school learning new information and skills while reviewing old ones. Thus, most of the topics are reinforced in succeeding grades, with students' exposure to the topic becoming wider and deeper. The following chart, based on the objectives for each lesson, illustrates the scope of topics and the sequence in which they are presented.

Information	7–9	10–12
dangers of unknown substances		
drugs and their effects	X	X
definition of drug	X	X
chemical dependency and the individual		X
chemical dependency in the family	X	X
alcohol	X	X
nicotine	X	X
marijuana	X	X
look-alike stimulants	X	X
cocaine		X

(continued)

Information *(continued)*

	7–9	10–12
other drugs		X
reasons why people use and don't use drugs	X	
risk factors and ways to reduce risks	X	X
identification and evaluation of sources of information about drugs	X	
drug advertisements	X	X
drugs causing problems in future as well as in present		X
factors which influence effects	X	
non-stereotypical description of drug users	X	
basic properties of cancer cells	X	
fetal alcohol syndrome	X	X
abusers hurting others	X	X
driving and drugs	X	X
sidestream smoke		X
drug-related emergencies		X
control of substances by federal schedules		X
sexuality and drugs		X
early warning signs of drug abuse		X
action on drug-related issues		X

Skills

	7–9	10–12
asking someone for something		
abiding by ground rules for discussing sensitive topics in front of others	X	X
making decisions	X	
asking someone to do something (assertiveness)		
keeping out of trouble (self-control)		
identifying sources of influence		
saying no to keep friends	X	X
making friends	X	
stopping enabling		X
intervening with friends		X
recognizing when to refer people to others		X
making referrals		X
teaching refusal skills		X

Bonding to School and Family

	7–9	10–12
explaining that problems are normal		
acknowledging feelings and dealing with them		
helping others feel included		
appreciating self as special	X	X
identifying ways to take care of the body		
identifying healthy ways to have fun	X	X
identifying personal strengths		
identifying others' strengths	X	
identifying sources of self-assessment		
assessing self		
recognizing power of saying no		

(continued)

Bonding to School and Family *(continued)*	7–9	10–12
recognizing the influence of stress		
identifying stressful situations and dealing with them		
asking for advice from a trusted person		
giving positive self-talk	X	X
giving affirmations to others	X	X
identifying what is important to self		
learning what is important to others		
identifying and building relationship with someone admired		
getting feedback about personal qualities		
understanding group pressures		
discussing adolescent concerns	X	
identifying feelings about drugs, dependency		X
responding to people without using stereotypes		X

POLICY ON DRUGS AND ALCOHOL

Essential to the development and implementation of a drug/ alcohol prevention, intervention and treatment program is the formulation and adoption by the board of education of a policy on drug and alcohol use. The policy protects the staff by making it clear who is to do what, under what conditions. The policy makes it clear to students that drug and alcohol use will not be tolerated and what the consequences will be if they break the rules. The very existence of a clear policy is an initial step in assisting students to resist negative peer pressure. In schools in which it is recognized that penalties will be imposed for drug/alcohol use, it gives students another valid excuse for saying "no."

Policy needs to be built on federal and state law and precedent cases. In general, all boards of education have the responsibility for the health and safety of students. All states have laws concerning the use and distribution of controlled substances. Cases heard by the Supreme Court have also clarified the rights of schools, for example, to conduct searches when there are "reasonable grounds" for suspicion that a student has violated the law or school rules. The Comprehensive Crime Control Act of 1984, makes it a federal crime to sell drugs in or near a school. Before developing a policy and procedures, state laws should be reviewed. In many states the Department of Education has gathered the pertinent laws together and made them available to school districts. Some states have mandated that districts adopt a policy concerning the use of controlled substances and have developed model policies. Whether a district starts from scratch or adapts/adopts a state sample policy, the district solicitor should review the policy before it is adopted by the board of education.

The policy should make explicit:

- that drug/alcohol use will not be tolerated
- that it is the staff's responsibility to act on information concerning drug/alcohol use by students
- that the staff will be "held harmless" for reporting information concerning the use or distribution of drugs/alcohol
- how, to whom and when information on drug/alcohol use or distribution is to be reported
- what procedures the school will follow to confirm the use or distribution of drugs
- if and how drug testing will be required and under what conditions
- drug/alcohol prevention curriculum requirements, grades K–12
- in cases of suspected distribution or sale, when and by whom the police will be informed
- that the use of drugs/alcohol by students constitutes a physical and mental risk to students and that information cannot be kept confidential and must be reported
- that not only do parents have the right to know that their child is suspected or known to be using a controlled substance, but they have the primary responsibility for treatment
- that lockers and personal possessions will be searched when there are "reasonable grounds" to suspect violations of school rules or laws
- what the school penalties will be for using, possessing, distributing or selling drugs/alcohol
- what requirements the board will make concerning assessment and treatment as a condition of re-entry into the school
- what assistance the school will make available to students concerned with drug/alcohol issues and for assistance during and after treatment
- what the roles of the Student Assistance Team, counselors, administrators, and nurses will be in confirming suspected drug/alcohol use, abuse, distribution, or sale
- what medical procedures should be followed if a student appears to be physically at risk

— what the relationship is between the schools and public and private agencies, treatment centers and hospitals

DRUG AND ALCOHOL GUIDELINES AND PROCEDURES

At the same time that the policy is being developed, detailed guidelines and procedures for implementing the policy should be devised. Working out the guidelines will help to determine if all aspects of the proposed policy can be implemented and if the policy is comprehensive enough to serve as a base for staff action. The guidelines should be reviewed by the board along with the policy, so that the board will understand exactly how the policy will be implemented.

The guidelines should list step-by-step procedures for the staff to follow under different circumstances, such as:

— when a staff member receives information that a student is under the influence of drugs/alcohol
— when staff observe a student who appears to be under the influence of drugs or alcohol
— when changes in student behavior over time suggest that a student has a problem which may be drug/alcohol related and is interfering with learning
— when a staff member sees a student use or has other evidence that a student has used alcohol or drugs in school
— when a staff member has information about or sees the transfer of drugs or alcohol
— when there appears to be a medical emergency regarding a student

The guidelines should take each potential triggering incident and list the actions, in sequence, that all the staff who may be involved need to take: how the student will be dealt with, how parents will be involved, how other agencies or the police will be involved. Very detailed guidelines and procedures help to answer the "what if?" questions of the staff. Even though the entire staff has been oriented to the policy and procedures and given copies, the individual teacher may not have any need to implement them for a long period of time. When he/she does have the occasion for use it is important that he/she has a reference which is perfectly clear about what is to be done. Detailed guidelines and procedures also help to clarify relationship questions, such as when the Student Assistance Team is involved, how and when the nurse takes part, what is the role of administration. A good way to test the proposed guidelines and policy is to develop several scenarios concerning drug/alcohol use in the school. Check to see if under the imagined circumstances each staff member who would be expected to play a role would know what he/she is to do. In the final analysis, every actual situation is different and, as the policy and guidelines are implemented, areas will be found which require changes or clarifications. Policy and guidelines should be reviewed at least once each year.

TRAINING THE STAFF

Once the policy and guidelines have been developed and approved it is essential that the staff be trained. Every staff member from administrator to custodian needs some training. The focus of the general training should be on recognition of possible drug/alcohol related situations and what the individual's role is under the guidelines. Staff such as administrators, counselors, nurses, and Student Assistance Team members will require much more detailed training in implementing the guidelines, in working with students with drug/alcohol problems, in working with parents and in working with agencies outside the school.

Orientation

Students and their parents need to be oriented to the policy and to the procedures which will be followed if drug/alcohol use is suspected and/or confirmed. The orientation for students should be both verbal and in written form. If possible, parents should also receive both oral and written orientation; however, at least parents should be sent written notification with copies of the policy and guidelines and a cover letter explaining why the school district has adopted the policy and guidelines, and a statement of intent to enforce.

APPLYING THE DRUG/ALCOHOL POLICY
IN A DISCIPLINE SITUATION

Policies and guidelines will vary based on individual differences among communities and variations in state law and regulation. However, discipline in drug/alcohol cases has three purposes:

- to serve as a deterrent for all students and the individual(s) involved in the incident

— to use the incident as a means for breaking through denial behaviors and getting help for the student

— to separate the student on drugs/alcohol from other students and the teachers at least for a while, thus reducing the negative effects on others and on learning

The most important application of the policy is the first application; the Board of Education has approved the policy and guidelines, the staff has been trained, the students and parents oriented; the stage is set and everyone is waiting to see if action will readily be taken. However, it may be weeks or months, rather than days or hours before there is an incident requiring discipline. The longer the time, the more important it becomes to review the procedures regularly with staff. If there is an incident and the procedures are not followed the entire program will lose at least some of its credibility.

How it Works—A Case Study
Drugs/Alcohol and Discipline

8:00 a.m.

A teacher enters the girls' room and smells a heavy, sweet smell which she suspects is marijuana. The teacher sees Sue, a tenth grade student, come out of a booth. Sue does not have a pass and is belligerent. The teacher checks the booth: the smell of marijuana is much stronger. Sue says she cut her "dumb math class." She slurs her words slightly.

8:10 a.m.

The teacher takes the student to the assistant principal. The nurse is called and she asks Sue some questions, such as, "Are you on any medication?" Sue says, "No." The assistant principal asks Sue if there were any other students in the girls' room while she was in there. Sue says, "No." He asks her to empty her pocketbook on his desk. Sue responds that she hasn't done anything. The assistant principal takes the pocketbook and empties the contents on his desk. An envelope with a tobacco-like substance is found and a package of cigarette papers. The suspicious items are placed in an envelope and sealed. The circumstances of where and how they were found are written on the envelope and dated. The assistant principal and nurse sign the envelope. Sue insists she was holding the items for a friend, but she will not say who. The assistant principal reminds Sue that under the policy, students are responsible for items in their possession or in their locker.

8:30 a.m.

Sue's mother is called to come to school. The juvenile officer is called and comes to pick up the evidence for testing.

10:00 a.m.

Sue's mother meets with the principal and assistant principal. Sue's mother explains that her daughter must just have been holding the things they found for some other student. The principal explains that there is reasonable evidence that Sue was using drugs and/or was in possession of controlled substances. He explains the policy and the procedures which will be followed:

- Sue is suspended for five days.
- Before she is readmitted to the school she must submit a physician's report stating that she has been examined for drug use within the following twenty-four hours. (A chronic user will show positive results for a long time. An occasional user will show positive urine results after use after 3 hours and up to 24 hours.) The report must state the results of the test and that the student is physically and mentally able to return to school.
- The principal provides Sue's mother with a list of community agencies who will do drug screening and assessment.
- The principal explains that in case there is a second offense, the penalty will be a minimum of ten day suspension, mandatory drug dependency assessment and a hearing before the school board concerning the possibility of expulsion.

Sue leaves with her mother. The teacher, nurse, assistant principal and principal write reports on the incident. The principal asks the Student Assistance Team to gather information concerning classroom actions from all of Sue's teachers and to discuss the findings.

2:00 p.m.

The juvenile officer calls to confirm that the substance in Sue's pocketbook was marijuana. The police will try to find out from Sue the source of the drug. The principal calls Sue's mother with the findings. The mother is still claiming her daughter was just holding the material for someone else. The principal holds to the steps which have been set forth.

3:00 p.m.

The principal confirms in writing to the parents what happened, actions taken, penalties imposed and requirements for readmission. A copy of the letter is sent to the superintendent. The action taken is verbally communicated to the teacher who identified the incident and took the original action.

TAKING ACTION IN SUSPECTED CASES
OF DRUG/ALCOHOL ABUSE

When disciplinary action is taken in a case of a student who is found to be under the influence of drugs/alcohol or in possession of a controlled substance, it is not unusual for other staff members to make statements like, "I knew that kid was on drugs, he was out of it most of the time in my class." If people knew, why didn't they take action? There are several reasons why staff members don't act or act in an ineffective way:

— They really don't "know" but only suspect substance abuse and are afraid they might be wrong.
— They are afraid that if they act they will not be supported by the administration and/or their colleagues.
— They are concerned that they might be the target of reprisals from students.
— They fear that they might be sued by parents.
— They have called parents in the past concerning what they observe in class, only to have the parent deny there is a problem.
— They have reported problems to administrators in the past and nothing has happened.

These are all reasons for teachers and administrators to hesitate in taking action. However, the earlier effective action can be taken in the case of suspected drug/alcohol abuse the better for the student involved and for other students in the building. The board-approved policy and guidelines for addressing suspected cases of drug/alcohol abuse are the first step in assuring the staff that there is commitment to solving the problem and there is support for the actions the staff takes under the policy and guidelines. The second step is to design the procedures so that action is taken in a concerted manner, when there is suspicion and before it becomes a discipline problem. The third step is to recognize that every action taken, even in cases where there is drug/alcohol addiction, will not be successfully concluded. Abuse and addiction problems carry with them huge amounts of denial on the part of the abuser, and frequently on the part of the parents. It may take several attempts to "break through" or abuse may have to get to the discipline stage before effective action is taken by the abuser or his/her parents. However, a well-planned team approach to identification, the gathering of descriptive behavior, and progressive degrees of confrontation, all with the aim of helping the student, will succeed in many cases.

INTERVENTION

Alcohol/drug addiction is a progressive disease which affects the person physically, socially, and mentally. If the destructive behavior pattern is not stopped it will lead to the inability to function and eventually to death. Addiction in an adolescent can develop in six months or even faster. It is uncertain why addiction is accelerated in children and teenagers. One theory is that the hypothalamus section of the brain which controls major portions of the physical and emotional actions of a person is still developing in adolescents and may be particularly sensitive to drugs/alcohol (Horton, 1985). Another possibility is that the child or adolescent has less experience in handling emotions, apparent crises, and peer pressures, and combined with emerging needs for independence, is emotionally at greater risk than adults. The initial experience with alcohol or drugs may be positive and lead to rapid acceleration of use. The earlier a child tries alcohol or drugs the more likely he/she is to become addicted. Students may begin by smoking cigarettes and then perhaps move on to alcohol and, not uncommonly, other drugs. However, for most teens the drug of choice and of addiction is alcohol. The earlier that there is effective intervention the better the chances are for successful arrest of the illness.

Alcohol/drug dependency is a primary condition. It must be dealt with before any other treatment for any other mental or physical problem can have long-term positive effects. The student may have emotional problems stemming from poor home environment, abuse, low self-esteem; however, the delusions and impaired judgment associated with addiction block efforts to deal with other problems (Johnson, 1980).

While individuals differ in terms of background, emotional makeup, experiences and exposure to life problems, the behaviors each exhibits as he/she is drawn into abuse and addiction to alcohol/drugs are quite predictable. As alcohol/drugs become a more dominant influence in a student's life observable changes occur in his/her behavior at home, with peers and in school. However, the chemically dependent person is so effective at denial and rationalization that he/she does not see the changes as problems. When problems are acknowledged, they are blamed on others.

The purpose of a formal intervention is to break through the defenses, the denial, the rationalization, and the projection in order to help the person. He/she cannot do this on his/her own. Attempts by parents or teachers to discuss the problem with the person usually fail – the person denies the problem, blames others or promises not to drink or "do drugs," only to break the promise. The chemically dependent person has impaired judgment; therefore, it takes extraordinary action to "break through." Information can only be received by the dependent person if it is presented in a receivable form. Vernon Johnson of the Johnson Institute in Minneapolis presents a set of seven rules to guide formal intervention (1980):

- The people involved in the intervention should be those who have influence on the person, such as parents, if they are willing to cooperate, or teachers, counselors and school administrators. In the case of chemically dependent adults, employers are frequently the most effective in breaking through to reality. In the case of a student, the school occupies roughly the same position as the employer does for an adult.
- As much information as possible concerning specific events should be collected and presented; generalizations should not be used.
- The data should be presented to the person in a way to show concern. The facts are presented to illustrate why there is concern.
- The descriptive behaviors should be tied to drinking or drug related behavior whenever possible. In the case of students and attempts at early intervention many of the facts will be those usually associated with alcohol/drug use. For example, a drop in grades, absenteeism, association with known alcohol/drug users.
- The information should be detailed and presented by more than one person.

— The goal is for the person who has been presented with an overwhelming dose of reality to, however grudgingly, accept reality and accept help.
— The options for help should be determined prior to the formal intervention, so that when the breakthrough occurs specific action can be taken.

Formal interventions are not emotionally easy on the student, parents or the staff. The staff who plan and carry out formal interventions must be trained, work with other staff in a group and have the support of administration and the board of education. The attempts at early intervention will not always succeed; however, because of the nature of the illness, there are no easy ways of getting the chemically dependent student help. The other options are: 1) to wait and hope someone outside the school recognizes the problem and is willing and capable of taking effective action, or 2) to wait until there is a crisis in the school which involves discipline or requires medical action and then to use the incident to force action on the chemical dependency problem.

TRAINING THE INTERVENTION TEAM

The Student Assistance Team or other group of staff members who are going to try to get assistance to a student prior to a student crisis need training. The team already possesses much of the knowledge needed for reviewing referrals and intervening with students and parents, teachers and administrators (see Chapter 5). The team is not going to attempt treatment. Its members are going to review the information concerning the student to determine if there are major changes in behavior. Teachers and administrators observe students every day and are well fitted to observe variations from the norm. The training needed to prepare them to intervene in suspected cases of chemical dependency include:

— acquiring background knowledge of the addiction process, progression of the disease, and usual approaches to treatment
— the reasons why "formal intervention" is needed to "break through" to assist a student
— how to collect, prepare and review data concerning a student
— how to conduct a "formal intervention"
— what treatment is available once there has been a breakthrough
— ways in which the school can help a student during or after treatment

The basic training can usually be accomplished in a few days. Counselors from local drug/alcohol treatment centers may be able to provide the training; also staff from other schools with Assistance Teams, or guidance counselors or psychologists on your own staff may have specific training in drug/alcohol intervention. In addition to the training, the team needs time to plan for the referral process, to role-play interventions and to plan how the program will be implemented.

How it Works—A Case Study
Suspected Drug/Alcohol Abuse

Following is a sample case study involving a suspected case of alcohol/drug abuse. It is assumed that the school has a Student Assistance Team; however, the guidance department could also function as a team with an administrator.

Tuesday Morning—Initial Referral

Mr. Smith, a teacher on the Student Assistance Team and the chairman of the team for the month, finds a referral from Mrs. Alverez, the physical education teacher, concerning Sue, an eleventh grade student (see sample referral form, pages 79–81).

Tuesday Afternoon—Team Meeting

The team reviews the form. Sue's grades have dropped from a "B" to a "C – "; she has asked to go to see the nurse several times in the past few weeks; she has "dropped" her previous group of friends and is now friendly with two senior girls who have had many discipline problems; she has been absent three Mondays in a row. Mrs. Alverez spoke to Sue about the changes she has noted. Sue says, "There is no problem, school is just a bore."

The team decides to gather information concerning Sue from all staff who have contact with her: teachers, the nurse, her basketball coach, the bus driver, the attendance officer, the assistant principal who handles discipline. A referral form with Sue's name on it and a note asking the staff member to return it within 24 hours is placed in an envelope and put in each staff member's box.

Thursday Afternoon—Team Meeting

The team reviews the information gathered from the staff. All of her teachers note that there have been observable changes in Sue's behavior—lower grades, late assignments, daydreaming or sleeping in class, sloppy dressing. The bus driver reports that Sue stopped taking the bus a couple of months ago. He noted on a couple of occasions that she was picked up at the bus stop by some kids in a car. The disciplinarian reports that Sue has had detention twice recently for being late to class. The nurse reports that when Sue comes to her office she has only vague complaints about feeling sick to her stomach. Sue has mentioned to the nurse that it is probably from "partying too much." The team decides that there is real cause for concern. Mrs. Fry, the guidance counselor (it could be any team member), is assigned to meet with Sue.

Friday Morning—Meeting with Sue

Mrs. Fry meets with Sue. She explains that Sue's teachers are concerned about her recent change in behavior and cites some of the changes noted by the staff. Mrs. Fry explains that the staff want to help Sue and she would like to hear what Sue has to say about what appears to be a problem. She cautions Sue, however, that any information she might share, which would represent a danger to Sue or to others, cannot be kept confidential. Sue denies there is any real problem, she is just bored with school. She is just like "all the other kids," she parties some on weekends and doesn't always feel like doing homework. Mrs. Fry asks her if she uses alcohol or drugs. Sue says, "You can't party if you don't drink, but they don't get drunk or anything." Sue says, "They never use drugs, just some 'joints' and occasionally some pills." Mrs. Fry asks Sue if she would be willing to complete a questionnaire. Sue says, "sure." She completes some of the questionnaire, but avoids the questions concerning drugs; she answers "yes" to a question concerning use of alcohol. Mrs. Fry explains to Sue that she considers Sue's problems serious enough to meet with Sue's parents and that she is going to call them.

Mrs. Fry notifies the team chairman that there will be a meeting set up with Sue's parents. The chairman notifies the principal and the rest of the team. Mrs. Fry calls Sue's mother to set up an appointment, preferably with both parents after school. Mrs. Fry states that a number of Sue's teachers are concerned with changes they have noted in her behavior. Depending on the parent's response Mrs. Fry will meet with the parents with the team chairman, or the entire team will meet with the parents and Sue.

Option #1

Sue's mother is glad the school called, she and her husband have also seen the changes in Sue, they have talked to her. Sue stole her little sister's allowance and they disciplined her, but nothing seems to help. She and her husband will be glad to meet with Mrs. Fry and anyone else who might help. The parents come in, discuss the findings of the team and are told that the team recommends that the parents take Sue for drug/alcohol assessment. Mrs. Fry provides the names and telephone numbers of two local assessment and treatment centers to the parents and promises to work with the parents on the problem. If the parents wish, Mrs. Fry explains that a "formal intervention" can be set up with the team, parents and Sue, to help Sue "break through" the denial. If there is a confirmed problem, Mrs. Fry promises the parents that the school will work with Sue and her parents. For example, Sue's behavior in school will be closely monitored, parents will be notified of any infraction of the rules, the school will support the therapy.

Option #2

Sue's mother, in response to Mrs. Fry's call, becomes defensive or hostile. This is the reaction the staff dreads. However, this is where team action and carefully prepared data is essential. Denial can be very powerful. Mental health professionals frequently say that parents or an individual teacher are no match for a lying denying teenager. The only way the school is going to help the student is to break through the denial. The way they do that is by delivering one strong unified message that says: 1) there is a problem, 2) excuses don't count, 3) you need to get help. The message is delivered by presenting in extreme detail to the parents and the student, all the information gathered on the student. The purpose of this is to overwhelm the parents, and hopefully the student, break through the denial and get the student help. The team will be prepared to recommend assessment and the kind of help available (names, phone numbers, even tentative appointments). Consequences of not acting will be explained, such as disciplinary action if school rules are broken and possible long-term effects on the student and the parents.

Not all confrontations work the first time around. However, in cases where they do not work (denial is not broken through and help is not provided) there is every likelihood that the student's behavior will result in disciplinary actions which may provide the base for a future successful confrontation and treatment.

Friday Afternoon—Team Meeting with Sue and Sue's Parents

The team chairman explains to Sue and her parents that there is a real concern about the changes in Sue's behavior in school and for Sue as a person. He asks that they listen to the observations and concerns in their entirety, and then the parents can ask questions and discuss ways of assisting Sue.

Each team member presents a part of the information collected, using dates, and specific incidents, for example:

Team member #1—reads a list of days and dates for the last three months that Sue was late to school or class.

Team member #2—reads a list of teacher comments including drops in grades, late assignments, actions in class.

Team member #3—reads the disciplinary action taken this year, detention, suspensions.

Team member #4—reports the visits to the nurse, the change in friends and the report of the bus driver concerning the fact that Sue has been observed being picked up in a car at the bus stop and has not ridden the bus for over a month.

Team member #5 (Mrs. Fry)—reports on her conversation with Sue, reporting Sue's statement that she does drink and parties and uses marijuana and pills occasionally. She shows the parents the partially completed questionnaire.

Sue denies everything. As far as she is concerned, the school is picking on her. She states that she doesn't have a drug or alcohol problem; everyone uses drugs; she can handle them and so can her friends. The mother is sure that there must be some mistake. She knows her daughter takes the bus because she isn't allowed to go to school in cars; besides none of her daughter's close friends have cars. The father blames the mother for not knowing what is going on.

After the initial outburst, the mother asks what can they do to help Sue or to find out if she needs help. The father says he doesn't see how this could happen. Sue cries and says she can handle it, she doesn't need help.

The team suggests that the parents have Sue undergo a drug/alcohol assessment. They explain how to set it up, what it entails, and what if any costs may be involved. They assure the parents that, based on the outcome of the assessment, the school will work with the parents and the student, and if treatment is involved, with the treatment provider. When the parents ask how soon such an assessment can take place, the chairman tells the parents that they can take Sue to the assessment center right after the meeting, and if they wish he can go and make the call now. The parents agree.

Wednesday—Team Meeting

The chairman reports that he has talked to Sue's parents. Sue has entered a twenty-eight day residential treatment program based on the results of the assessment. The team puts the date of Sue's return to school on their calendar for follow-up action. Sue's parents tell the chairman that several of Sue's friends are also using alcohol and drugs. The team decides to gather data on these students.

TREATMENT

While the school is not directly involved in the treatment of chemical dependency problems, school personnel should know what treatment services are available in the area as well as the characteristics of effective adolescent programs and which local programs have those characteristics. When the problem is acknowledged by the parents and/or the student, they will want to know where to get help. The staff should be prepared with a list of options and be able to discuss at least briefly the program and the costs. Information can be summarized on a handout which can be made available to parents and students.

In addition, for staff to plan to work effectively with students during or after treatment, it is useful to understand the goals and forms of treatment provided by the various programs.

Assessment

The first step in treatment is assessment. The assessment will confirm the existence of a problem and the stage of chemical use and/or dependency. If the assessment confirms that the student is chemically dependent, outpatient or inpatient treatment will be recommended. Sometimes the assessment will be conducted during a three- to five-day stay in a hospital or treatment center; in other cases the assessment will be done as an outpatient. During this period, parents and siblings will also be interviewed. It is important that the facility used for assessment has experience with adolescents and that the staff has specific training in adolescent dependency problems. When possible, permission should be obtained from parents to share the information gathered by the school with the assessment agency.

It is not unusual for parents or students, when confronted with the examples of the student's negative behavior, which is usually linked to chemical dependency, to explain that the student is seeing a psychiatrist. In some cases the student may have been in "treatment" for some time. It is also not unusual to learn that the student and the parents attribute at least part of the student's behavior to the prescription drugs provided by the doctor. This is a delicate situation for the staff. If chemical dependency is a "primary" disease, as most professionals in the field believe, it must be treated directly before other problems can be addressed. Many psychiatrists have not had specific training in treating chemical dependency and focus on trying to determine "why" the adolescent has developed certain behaviors and attitudes. In order to help the student cope with day-to-day pressures, drugs are prescribed. Sometimes these prescribed drugs are then supplemented by illegal drugs or alcohol. As tactfully as possible, the staff should try to determine the focus of the current treatment.. If the focus is not on chemical dependency, then they should suggest that the student be assessed in a program which specializes in adolescent chemical dependency problems. According to Dr. Mark Gold of Fair Oaks Hospital, more people die from the misuse of prescribed drugs each year than from all illegal drugs combined (1986).

Inpatient Treatment

Inpatient treatment includes:
- observation and detoxification (if necessary)
- therapy to help the person identify the illness as a disease and accept the illness
- medical treatment if necessary
- introduction to the Twelve-Step Program of Alcoholics Anonymous
- development of a rehabilitation plan

Patients participate in:
- education programs aimed at gaining greater understanding of the disease and its effects
- group therapy with others with the same problems in order to break down defenses and negative attitudes
- individual and family counseling to deal with the particular life problems of the patient and the family

Following the inpatient treatment the person will continue in a program of outpatient treatment and will attend AA meetings.

Usually inpatient treatment programs last twenty-eight days. This period of time allows for detoxification (if necessary) and the establishment of the therapy program. There is no magic number of days that apply to all patients; however, from a pragmatic point of view most programs are twenty-eight days long because that is the period of time most insurance plans will cover.

If possible, the staff that will be involved in identifying options to parents and students should visit local facilities to get a better idea of the services provided. Some of the characteristics to consider are:

— Is there a separate program for adolescents?
— What is the experience of the staff in working with adolescents?
— Does the program include education, group and individual therapy?
— Is there a post-treatment plan developed in detail?
— If you can talk to patients, do those near the end of their stay think the program was worthwhile?
— Will the facility take any patients that cannot afford to pay or who do not have insurance?

Another factor which parents should consider in selecting a treatment facility is location. There are a number of outstanding programs across the country with well-deserved reputations. Parents want the best for their children; however, follow-up treatment is essential. If a student goes to a program in another state or even within the state but far from home, follow-up may be very difficult. The parents will have to weigh the advantages and disadvantages of local versus distant facilities.

Outpatient Treatment

Another option is outpatient care. The stigma of hospitalization is avoided and the expense is less. In the case of intranasal cocaine users, the sudden stopping of use usually does not require management of physical withdrawal problems. In the cases of tranquilizers, alcohol or use of mixed drugs, withdrawal may need to be handled in a hospital setting.

An outpatient program should require complete and immediate abstinence from the use of all drugs. The program should include routine urine testing throughout the treatment program, in the initial stages at least twice a week. The program should have a complete treatment plan which includes:

Part I—The aim is to have the patient drug-free for at least a month. During this period he/she sees a professional almost every day. The program parallels the inpatient program of education, support and counseling, and involves attendance at self-help groups like Alcoholics Anonymous or Cocaine Anonymous.

Part II—The aim is to prevent relapse and to handle relapse if it occurs. Adults are counseled to avoid people and places that are likely to trigger the return to drugs. Adolescents have a particularly difficult time since they cannot avoid school or usually, the people with whom they used drugs. Unfortunately, changing schools does not help much since it is easy for a student to find other students who use drugs/alcohol in virtually any school. Parents and siblings play an extremely important part in the recovery process and should be included in counseling and group therapy. Urine testing should be continued. Even in well-planned programs and with the support of all those involved, it is not unusual for the student to have a relapse. It is important for guilt to be controlled and the program to be resumed.

Part III—The last phase begins usually after the first year and continues indefinitely, since the chemically dependent person is not cured but recovering. Continuing support is needed to handle difficult times and situations.

THE SCHOOL'S ROLE IN AFTERCARE

The school can play an effective part after the assessment for chemical dependency has been made and treatment has been initiated. Even in cases where the student has only been experimenting with drugs/alcohol, the school can play a constructive part.

The first role of the school is to continue the strict application of the school rules, not only concerning drug/alcohol abuse but all school rules. The student needs the structure the rules require as well as knowledge of the consequences. Parents need to be kept informed concerning breaches of the rules and notified immediately when there are unexplained absences or class cuts.

Another role of the school is to assist in the treatment plan as it affects activities in the school. While it is difficult for students to avoid other students who have been associated with their problem, there may be cases when changes in academic schedules may be helpful.

Remediation of academic deficiencies may be needed in the case of some students, since while they were involved in drugs/alcohol, there was a lessening of interest in school and frequently a reduced ability to concentrate. The student may need tutoring in several subjects. The school staff can help to arrange the tutoring and monitor the progress. If the student works part-time, it may be useful for him/her to pay for at least part of the tutoring. In the past the income probably went to purchase drugs/alcohol; paying for the tutoring is an illustration of the cost of his/her actions and reduces the chances that the funds will be used for negative purposes.

While the school is not in the treatment business, group sessions led by trained leaders which focus on school-related issues can be very helpful. With adults who experience chemical dependency, therapists try to build on the life skills the adult had prior to the dependency. Adolescents who have had as their focus alcohol/drugs for some period of time may not have any useful life experiences or skills to recall that will help them with the general problems of their age group. In many cases their social and psychological development appears to have been "frozen" at an earlier stage. They may never have asked for a date when they were not high, and dates may have been only excuses for getting high. They may be very uncomfortable around "straight" kids and not know what they do for a good time. Lying to cover their actions may be so ingrained that they continue to lie out of habit.

The school group which consists of other students with similar problems provides an opportunity for sharing the difficulties associated with return to school and the development of non-drug/alcohol using peers. The group should meet a minimum of one day a week. There should be two leaders, one male and one female, who have some training in facilitating the group process, empathy for the students, knowledge enough that they do not become "enablers," and the ability to keep the group focused on school-related issues. Guidance counselors may already be trained in the group process and may only need training in the aims of the group and the essentials of drug/alcohol dependency and recovery. Members of the Student Assistance Team may have the background in chemical dependency problems and need only some training in facilitating a group. In schools where such groups are functioning, participation in the group may be part of the requirements for returning to school. The existence of the group should also be made known to the treatment facilities in the area, so the group can be considered in the development of treatment plans. Treatment facilities in the area may also be willing to assist in establishing the group and in training the leaders.

The successful recovery of an adolescent involved with drugs/ alcohol requires the coordinated effort of those most closely associated with the student, plus the student's own desire to eliminate drugs/alcohol from his/her life. The school and the school environment is a central player in the life of the adolescent and therefore, a potentially effective force in assisting the student during the recovery period.

SUMMARY

This chapter dealt with the abuse of drugs and alcohol and the role of the school in prevention, assistance, confrontation and aftercare. Guidelines were established for developing policy and operational procedures.

Strategies for managing drug/alcohol discipline cases and suspected drug/alcohol abuse cases were presented in detail and illustrated by case studies. The role of the school in aftercare was discussed.

CHAPTER 7

Suicide Prevention and Postvention

WHY THE SCHOOL HAS A ROLE IN SUICIDE PREVENTION

Professional educators have a moral, humanitarian and legal responsibility to safeguard student health.

Students are in school 6–7 hours a day. Teachers and other staff are in an excellent position to identify students who are at risk. Parents may have one teenager at home; teachers have hundreds of teenagers against which to gauge the behaviors of a particular teenager.

As the following statistics indicate, the odds are overwhelming that an attempted or successful suicide will affect every secondary school.

- Five hundred thousand teenagers each year will make a suicide attempt serious enough to require medical attention.
- Between 4000–5000 teenagers will commit suicide each year.
- For every one who commits suicide, one hundred will make the attempt.
- Girls attempt suicide ten times more often than boys.
- Boys complete suicide five times more often than girls.
- Drugs and alcohol are involved in two out of three suicides.
- Every 90 minutes an adolescent commits suicide (Bolton, 1986).

Students who are in enough psychological pain to consider suicide are not going to gain from regular class instruction.

Schools may be legally liable for failure to identify and act in cases of students-at-risk (New Haven Superior Court, *New York Times,* Feb. 8, 1987).

School staff, policies, procedures and curriculum can reduce the risk of suicide.

THE ROLE OF THE SCHOOL IN SUICIDE PREVENTION

The basic role of the school staff is to observe behavior, identify warning signals, follow established school procedures, notify parents, refer for treatment, and support the student during and after treatment. The responsibility of the school is not therapy.

In order to carry out the role of the school effectively, the following steps should be taken:

— Establish a policy
— Establish procedures
— Provide all staff with training on identification of warning signs and procedures to follow
— Identify skilled staff or train a team of staff to act on referrals
— Identify and make contact with agencies which can provide treatment
— Develop an after-attempt support program
— Assess the school environment to identify actions or lack of actions which may contribute to student pain

POLICY ON SUICIDE PREVENTION

A fundamental responsibility of the staff of the school, both professional and non-professional, is the safety of students. The staff has the responsibility to act on any information which indicates that a student is in danger. The administration has the responsibility for establishing procedures for acting on information. The school board has the responsibility to establish a policy which makes explicit:

— that procedural guidelines for handling situations which may result in self-inflicted harm to students are in place
— that staff will be "held harmless" for reporting information on potential suicide
— that in the case of a student at risk of committing suicide, the staff cannot guarantee confidentiality and that even if such a guarantee was given, the responsibility of the staff is to share the information with appropriate others, including administration and parents
— that parents have not only the right to know that their child

may be at risk but also the primary responsibility to provide for any treatment

— that the school has the responsibility to gather information, including that from the child, concerning possible suicide
— that the school has responsibility for ongoing support of the student at risk, within the usual resources of the school
— that the school will cooperate, within its resources, with parents and treatment agencies in assisting the child at risk

SUICIDE PREVENTION GUIDELINES AND PROCEDURES

Specific procedures should be developed that clearly spell out "who" is to do "what," "where," and "when" if there is any risk of suicide. In priority order the general process must address: 1) safety of the student, 2) communication with those in a position to help, 3) referral, treatment and follow-up. Since the initial information coming to a staff member may range from a general uneasiness, based on a student essay, to a friend of the child at risk telling the teacher that "John says he is going to kill himself with his father's gun," the procedures have to have several levels of action. In addition, there should be alternatives in terms of "who" will do "what." It is not always possible that one person will be available or one person will always play a particular role. Following is a set of sample procedures for a high school (middle schools, junior high schools and elementary schools with grades five and above should also have established procedures). It is recommended that the administration have the district solicitor review proposed policy and guidelines before they are adopted. In this example, it is assumed that the school has a guidance staff, a student assistance team (nurse, teachers, administrator, counselor) and a district psychologist. If a district does not have all of these positions, other staff members and even resources from outside the school can be substituted.

Suicide Prevention Procedures—An Example

I. Responsibility of All District Staff

a. Any information which indicates that a student may be considering suicide must be reported to the principal, a member of the student assistance team (counselor, teacher, administrator, nurse) or the director of guidance. In the case of potential danger to a student there can be no confidentiality.

b. If the staff member believes that the student may be at immediate risk, then the staff member should stay with the student and send another teacher or a student to get help, or bring the student to the guidance office or nurse's office.

c. A student who is considered at risk should not be allowed to leave the school until further determination can be made concerning the degree of risk.

d. If information concerning a student at risk comes to a staff member outside of the school hours, the staff member shall attempt to reach the principal, counselor, or team member. If they are unavailable the staff member should try to reach the student's parents. In the case where a plan to commit suicide may be evident (a letter received by the teacher saying goodbye, or a phone call from a friend of the student outlining a suicide plan), and if parents cannot be reached, the police should be called.

e. After the safety of the student has been considered and the appropriate people notified, the staff member will complete an "At-Risk Student Form" and file it with the principal.

II. Principal, Student Assistance Team, Counselor, Psychologist

a. The principal, student assistance team member, a designated counselor or the psychologist will interview the student and develop his/her opinion concerning the degree of suicide risk.

b. If after the interview the person feels uncomfortable concerning how serious or immediate the threat is the person should call a team meeting to discuss the situation and make a decision.

III. High-Risk Student

The high-risk student is one who admits he/she is contemplating suicide, has tried to kill himself/herself before, has a plan for how he/she could kill himself/herself, has the means for carrying out the plan, sees life as hopeless, sees death as a way out the pain, has a new burden added to an already bleak view of life, has given away possessions. It is not necessary for the student to fit all these categories to be considered high risk. The principal, Student Assistance Team member, counselor or psychologist will arrange for the following:

a. That the student is not left alone
b. That parents are to be notified immediately to come to school
c. That the area Crisis Center should be contacted and a tentative appointment for the student and parents set up
d. That the staff member who interviewed the child and the principal meet with the parents and the child to share the information and recommended action to be followed
e. That the counselor or Student Assistance Team member facilitates the connection of the parents and student with the Crisis Center
f. That the child leaves school only with a parent, guardian, or parent- or guardian-appointed person or mental health professional
g. That a staff member follows up the next day with the parents to determine what action was taken and to clarify the role of the school
h. That brief information concerning the outcome of the initial referral is shared with the staff member who made the referral. If the situation is general knowledge, then brief information should be shared with all staff
i. If in the course of the interview or from other sources it is suggested that the means to commit suicide have been brought to school, it will be considered grounds for "reasonable search" of the student or his/her locker or another student's locker, if indicated
j. That the counselor or Student Assistance Team will provide ongoing school support, if possible in cooperation with the primary treatment agency or mental health professional

IV. Moderate-Risk Student

The student does not see hope for life to improve, admits that he/she has thought about suicide, doesn't have a plan for how he/she might commit suicide, feels that he/she has at least one friend or person he/she feels close to, there has not been a major new stress (only friend just moved away, broke up with girl friend), doesn't have easy access to means of committing suicide, there has been no radical change in behavior. The principal, Student Assistance Team member, a counselor or the psychologist will be responsible for the following:
a. Notification of the parents

b. Monitoring the activity of the student during the day
c. Meeting with the parents and the student and facilitating contact with a crisis intervention counselor or center
d. Providing the parents and student with information on emergency services in the community
e. Arranging ongoing school support, if possible in cooperation with the primary referral agency or mental health professional

V. Low-Risk Student

General sense of unhappiness, some withdrawal, writing which is depressing or focuses on death, change in classroom behavior, change in appearance, withdrawal from some school activities, no specific indicators that death is being considered. The principal, Student Assistance Team member, counselor or psychologist will be responsible for the following:

a. The Student Assistance Team will gather additional information from all the staff who interact with the student (see form, pages 79–81).
b. The Student Assistance Team will review this information and the interview results and decide if parents should be presented with the findings.
c. Meeting with the parents and student, if necessary, to discuss the concern and possible avenues of help
d. Encouraging the student to talk with parents about his/her problems, volunteering to meet with the parents if the student would like that course of action
e. Developing a plan for assisting the student in school and for monitoring, since young people can move quickly from low risk to high risk as situations change.

VI. Important Telephone Numbers

School extensions
The following telephone numbers and extensions will be available in each classroom:
    Principal: 201
    Guidance: 313
    Assistance Team: 413
    Psychologist: 110
Crisis Center:
    Dr. Jones: 555-1234

Ms. Smith: 555-4321
Hospital:
   Town General: 555-7777
Police:
   Sgt. Conner: 555-2222

TRAINING THE STAFF

There are two types of training which are required. The first involves all staff (including secretaries, aides and bus drivers). The training can be held during regular faculty meetings or during in-service sessions. The training should include the following:

- a brief background concerning the need (a few of the statistics)
- why the staff should be involved in identification and intervention
- what the role of the staff is and is not
- policy of the board of education
- in-depth review of procedures to follow if warning signs are identified (Copies of the procedures should be distributed with lists of contact staff.)
- confidentiality vs. student safety (Never promise confidentiality.)
- myths concerning suicide
- warning signs (Distribute a list as well as discuss the topic.)

The second type of training involves those to whom identified at-risk students will be reported. They should include administrators, counselors, nurse, student assistance team, school psychologist. Training of these individuals will require considerably more time and the services of an experienced trainer. The trainer might come from a Suicide Crisis Center, an Adolescent Treatment Center, or your own school psychologist may be qualified and willing to do the training. In addition to the general staff education outlined above, the training should include:

- interviewing the identified student
- handling confidentiality concerns of the at-risk student and others who provided information (The student's safety is first.)
- discussing the situation with parents alone and with the parents and the student
- presenting and discussing alternative assistance available to

parents (A typed resource sheet should be made available to parents and student.)
- suggesting the ways in which the school can assist and support the student and parents

While all the staff identified as working in a student assistance capacity should be trained, it is possible that not all these individuals will feel comfortable interviewing students identified as at-risk. Those staff members who are comfortable with the role should be identified and should be the ones who will conduct the interviews. Other team members can play other roles in the assistance process.

Another group that the school staff may want to orient are parents in general. Suicide prevention could be the topic for a home and school session. The session might cover the following:
- reasons for concern
- warning signs (handout)
- assistance available at school and in the community (handout)
- overview of school policy and procedures

COMMUNITY RESOURCES

In most areas a wealth of services are available to the school, students and families. However, the services of even similar sounding agencies may vary tremendously. At a time of crisis, the staff which meets with parents needs to know which services are appropriate and available. The board of education may want officially to designate one or more agencies as approved referrals. The staff needs to know the exact nature of services provided, how children are entered into the program or receive services, costs and insurance acceptance policies, availability of services (24 hrs a day, three-month waiting list), emphasis on adolescent treatment and names of contact persons. A staff member should visit the major service agencies to discuss and, if possible, view programs. It is very disconcerting to be in a crisis situation with a student and parents and find out the help that you thought to be available has evaporated. Since two out of three suicides involve drug and/or alcohol, identified resources should also be equipped to provide drug and alcohol assessment and treatment services if at all possible. If the district has a social worker, he/she may already be familiar with community agencies and can help put together a resource list.

Every person who may be in the position of meeting with students and parents concerning possible suicide should have a copy of the services list readily available and have extra sheets for the student and family.

THE SCHOOL'S ROLE AFTER A SUICIDE ATTEMPT

The problems which led a student to consider or attempt suicide do not go away when the problem is identified and outside assistance secured. The student remains at-risk of suicide for at least two years and maybe for life. A particular life situation may have triggered an actual attempt or heightened the risk, but the immediate situation has to be combined with inadequate life coping skills and ongoing problems in order to escalate into a crisis. The school is not in the therapy business but can provide a post-crisis support program. Such a program can take a number of forms to address the following:

a. Transition back into the school
b. Monitoring of the student
c. Support in school related matters

Transition Back Into School

Even if only a few staff members knew that the student was at-risk, that his parents were called in and that treatment was recommended, there will be a certain degree of awkwardness experienced by the student when he/she returns to school. If the student made an actual attempt and it is general knowledge, return to school will be even more of a problem.

The transition plan should have the following elements:

– A counselor should be assigned to coordinate post-crisis support for the student, parents, treatment agency, teachers as necessary and the administration. The student should know the counselor will be available, if needed.
– There should be discussion with classroom teachers concerning the student's return to class. In general, the academic expectations for the child should remain the same as for other children. A consistent structure is important. If the student has been out for a long period of time, a reasonable schedule for makeup and tutoring will have to be developed.

— If the parents and the treatment agency are willing, a support plan should be discussed with the therapist.

Monitoring

Students who have been identified as at-risk or who have attempted suicide should continue to be monitored when they return to school. The purpose of the monitoring is:

— to identify any changes in behavior which might signal a heightening of risk
— to identify and provide support in cases where the school may be contributing negatively to readjustment
— to identify opportunities for the staff to support the student

The counselor in charge of the student should check with teachers and other staff on a regular basis and with the student as well. Care, however, should be taken not to cause further embarrassment to the student or make the monitoring an added source of stress.

After Suicide Attempt Support Group

Unfortunately, it is not unusual for a high school to have identified several students at medium or high risk for suicide and to have several students who have made some form of a suicide attempt. A school support group run by a male and a female group leader can help to reduce the stress related to school and peers. Such a group is not a therapy group nor should it take the place of outside professional help. However, meeting with other students to discuss school related situations, problems and strategies can provide support for students at-risk. Such groups might be run by guidance staff, the school psychologists, interested teachers or Student Assistance Team member. Training needs to be provided for the group leaders and there needs to be a clear understanding of what the group is and is not. Such a group might meet once or twice a week.

ASSESSING THE SCHOOL ENVIRONMENT

Suicides do not occur because a student failed a test or didn't make the team. Such episodes may constitute the "final straw" or even be cited by the student as "the" reason. However, the reasons why a student attempts or seriously considers suicide are much more complex. The school can reduce the risk of suicide through awareness, caring and action, but it can not eliminate the possibility of suicide.

One positive action a school staff can take is to scan the school environment to identify negative stress points. For example, transition to high school is a time of stress for most students. What can be done to ease the transition? What can be eliminated? Is there informal hazing of freshmen? Can this be replaced by the assigning of an upper classman to assist each freshman? Can peer counseling groups be established? Are sports and extracurricular activities inclusive or exclusive in nature? How can activities be modified in order to better meet the needs of students?

Another positive action a school can take is to review and, if necessary, revise curriculum. Suicide prevention cannot be taught directly to students. Health and other areas of the curriculum can, however, be used to teach life skills such as decision making, communications, and human relations, which will help students deal effectively with problems.

POSTVENTION—SUICIDE OR SUSPECTED SUICIDE

It is said there are only two types of schools—ones which have had a student commit suicide, and ones which will have a student commit suicide. Sometimes it is clear immediately when a student (or staff member) dies that suicide was the cause. For example, a note is left or the manner in which he/she died clearly indicates suicide. More often, some of the negative aspects of the death, such as evidence of drug overdose or automobile death involving alcohol, separate it from death "from natural causes," such as disease. Knowing the cause of death or suspected cause of death is important for two reasons:

- It is necessary to be honest about the death with students and faculty.
- If it is a suicide, rumored suicide, or possible accidental suicide, it is necessary that this form of death not be glorified as a means for solving problems.

Most of the information and suggested procedures which follow would also be appropriate for handling the aftermath of a death of a student or staff member regardless of the cause.

GUIDELINES FOR RESPONDING TO SUICIDE

Do's

— Get available facts about the death from the police or family.
— Develop a plan for the day which includes who is going to do what, how and when (the best time to develop at least an outline of a plan is before it is ever needed).
— Communicate quickly and honestly with staff and students concerning the death.
— Maintain the school schedule.
— Provide support for the following groups:
  – close friends of the deceased
  – the teachers and students who would have been in class with the deceased student that day (dealing with the empty desk)
  – faculty members who may have been close to the student, who may feel they should have been able to have prevented the death (the morbid essay found by the teacher but not read until after the writer's death); or, in the worse case, where a staff member is blamed by the student for the actions he/she took (e.g., a suicide note citing being cut from a team as the reason for the suicide)
  – other students in the school who may not have known the deceased student well but are emotionally at risk
  – the faculty as a whole
  – the student body as a whole
— Communicate with other administrators in the district. Give priority to principals who may have siblings of the deceased in their schools.
— Designate one person to be the official contact for information and let people know who it is.
— Develop a plan for the following month including the day of the viewing, the day of the funeral, days of special events which would have included the deceased, handling students with delayed or prolonged reactions.

Don'ts

— Don't let students who may be upset go home unless the parents come for them (parents should know what has happened) and someone will be home with them.
— Don't announce the death on the PA system.
— Don't modify the school schedule.
— Don't plan a school memorial service.

Plans and Actions

When the school is notified that a death has occurred, action must be taken quickly. When a detailed plan exists, the school is ready to go into action. If there is no plan, there is not much time to plan and act. The following is presented as a case study; it is a step-by-step description of the actions a school might take in an actual situation. While each situation and each school is slightly different the case study can serve as a guide for action.

How it Works—A Case Study
The Suicide of a Student

7:30 a.m.—Monday

A student tells the assistant principal that John, a senior student, died Sunday morning probably because of an overdose of pills. The assistant principal meets immediately with the principal.

7:40 a.m.

The Principal makes the following calls:
- Parents—A distraught parent confirms that John was found dead in bed Sunday morning, there was an empty pill bottle by the bed and the police have been there. The principal asks who John's closest friends were, expresses condolences and hangs up.
- Police—Police confirm that there was an empty bottle of pills, but no suicide note and the exact cause of death cannot be confirmed until after the autopsy.
- Central Office—The principal notifies the superintendent.
- Middle School Principal—He notifies this principal because John's brother is a middle school student.

- Special Education Supervisor—He requests the services for the day of the school psychologist.

8:00 a.m.

Meeting in Principal's Office with Director of Guidance, Superintendent, Assistant Principals, Nurse, member of Student Assistance Team.

The principal outlines the plan for the day:

- A memo will be sent to all teachers before the beginning of third period. The memo will include the fact that John died, what is known about the death, where to send students who are visibly upset or request to leave the room, and an announcement of a faculty meeting at the end of the day. A sample memo follows.

East High School

TO: All Staff

FROM: George Brown, Principal

DATE: January 12, 1987

I regret to have to report to you that John Jones, a senior student, died at home Saturday night. Right now there is no confirmed cause of death. I request your cooperation in doing the following:

1. Please inform your third period students that John has died. I am sure you will appreciate the need to communicate this information as gently as possible.

2. If any student in your class is very upset, that youngster should be sent to the guidance office. Students should be told that counseling support will be provided during the day. Staff are also welcome to discuss their feelings and concerns with the guidance staff or myself throughout the day.

3. There will be a special meeting for all members of the staff at 2:15 in the auditorium.

- John's current teachers will be called to a meeting immediately following this meeting. The school psychologist and assistant principal will meet with them and discuss ways of handling the death with their classes.
- Guidance counselors, psychologist and Student Assistance Team members will meet to set up procedures for counseling students. All close friends will be called down, students sent by teachers or requesting counseling will be seen, any student coming to the nurse will also be seen by a

counselor. If parents come to pick up a student the counselor will speak to the parents before they leave with the child. A staff member will be in the guidance conference room all day to direct students to specific counselors. Team members and counselors will be visible and available in the cafeteria during lunch.

- The nurse will determine if any visits to the nurse's office are related to the death. Students will see a counselor and will be encouraged to stay in school. No students will be allowed to go home unless picked up by parents who will be home with them.
- The parents of any student counseled or sent to the nurse because of reaction to the death will be called during the day to tell them of the death and their child's concern.
- The psychologist and the counselors will be available to any faculty member who wants to talk.
- All notes to leave school, for example to go to a doctor's appointment, will be verified before students are allowed to leave.
- Any information coming to the faculty concerning suicide risk or drug use by other students will be followed up, in accordance with established procedures (this may be a time when students are very open and an opportunity to get other students the help they need).

Staff Comments at the Meeting

- The nurse reports that two of John's friends have already come to the nurse's office with requests to go home. They are now with their counselors. A very upset student who barely knew John is in the nurse's office and wants to go home. He is lying down and his counselor will see him in a few minutes.
- The guidance staff reports several students have already come down to see their counselor and two faculty members have been in.

8:30 a.m. Meeting

The psychologist and assistant principal meet with John's teachers. Suggestions are made concerning telling the class. If any students are very upset they should be sent to the Guidance Conference room. Teachers should use their own judgment concerning how much discussion of the death they encourage.

Teachers should stress how tragic and permanent death is. Students will not be encouraged to speculate or to advance unconfirmed rumors.

8:40 a.m. Meeting

The guidance staff (except one who is covering the office), available Student Assistance Team members, psychologist and social worker meet to schedule coverage of guidance center and to work out details. Those not in attendance will be informed by a specific person who is present.

9:00 a.m. Memo to Staff

The memo is sent to each staff member asking him/her to announce the death and procedures for the day at the beginning of third period (see page 124).

8:00 a.m. Crisis Consultant

The principal calls the local crisis center and requests a counselor to meet with staff at the end of the day and to discuss ways the faculty can support each other and students during the period following the death. Also, the staff should be told what not to do (this can be done by the principal or counselor but it may have better impact coming from an outside person who is trained specifically to handle these situations and who may be more comfortable conducting the session).

8:00 a.m. to 2:05 p.m.

The plan is in action and regular school activities continue.

2:15 p.m. Faculty Meeting

- The principal gives a review of the day, actions taken by the school, update on information concerning the death, and accepts comments from the staff.
- The crisis consultant gives an overview of suicide and provides recommendations on how the staff should respond to the situation in the next few days (note: review in detail with consultant how it was handled), along with suggestions for staff on handling the next month (business as usual, deal with individual problems as they arise). Days of particular significance (the viewing, funeral, student's birthday) should be considered in advance. If the student was a senior, a big test should not be scheduled the day of the funeral; on the other hand, freshmen may not know the

student at all and no modifications need to be made. Remember, the structured schedule of the day is, in itself, a support for students and teachers. Students who want to should go to the viewing or funeral, but a memorial service in the school should not be held because the student shouldn't be made a role model. An in-school memorial service tends to do this and it is also separated from the reality that he/she is really dead, while attendance at a viewing or funeral keeps in perspective that death is final.

HANDLING THE GRIEF OF THE SUICIDE SURVIVORS

In addition to the usual feelings of grief which follow the death of a friend or associate, those who were close to the suicide victim frequently experience feelings of guilt and sometimes anger. Survivors lament, "If only I had called him." "If only I hadn't been so blind to the clues." Another reaction can be one of anger. "How could he leave me? Why didn't he trust me to help?"

Survivors need to talk out their feelings. They need to come to the realization that even if they had been there on the particular night when the suicide occurred, someone who was determined to kill him-/herself would have just picked another time. They need to understand that anger is also part of grief. They need to come to the realization that the suicide was an escape from intolerable pain for the victim.

It takes time for survivors to learn to handle their reactions. They should be encouraged to get involved with others and to return to routine living. In many cases new routines need to be established, since interaction with the victim was part of the old routine.

In addition, since so many teen suicides involve drugs and/or alcohol, it is not uncommon for the friends of the victim to have drug/alcohol problems also. The suicide may increase the dependency of survivors on drugs and alcohol as they try and escape the reality of death. The suicide may also be the opportunity to "get through to friends" and get them the help that they may need.

SUMMARY

This chapter presented the steps school staff can take in preventing suicide. The extent of the problem; the role of the school; the development of policy, guidelines and procedures; the training of staff; and the transition back to school after an attempt were discussed.

Step-by-step procedures were detailed to assist school staff who have to deal with the suicide death of a student. Included are a sample memo to staff, plans, meeting agendas and suggestions for assisting students and staff to handle grief.

CHAPTER 8

AIDS—Prevention, Assistance

THE PROBLEM

The U.S. Centers for Disease Control (CDC) estimate that 20,000 people have Acquired Immunity Deficiency Syndrome (AIDS), 150,000 have AIDS-Related Complex and one million are asymptomatic carriers (Weiner, 1986).

In the school-age (6–18) group the CDC report only 59 cases of AIDS (Weiner, 1986). However, because of the long incubation stage of AIDS and the fact that people can carry and transmit the virus for years without themselves developing symptoms, many AIDS patients in the 19-year-old and above group may have contracted the disease at an earlier age. The adolescent years are years of experimentation. Unfortunately, experimentation with intravenous drug use and sex puts students at risk for AIDS.

HOW AIDS IS SPREAD

AIDS is a sexually transmitted disease. It can also be spread through the exchange of blood, as in sharing of needles in the use of drugs, or prenatally from mother to child. Now that the blood supply for transfusions is screened for AIDS, it is expected that new infection from transfusions will drop to near zero. Sexually, AIDS can be spread through both heterosexual and homosexual contact. It is not uncommon for school-age children to experiment with both heterosexual and homosexual sex. About half of all teenagers are sexually active before they leave high school (National Research Council, 1987). Kinsey (1948) estimated that more than 27% of males, 15 and under had experienced some homosexual activity (in Weiner, 1986). Students are also prone to experiment with drugs. While the drug of preference remains alcohol, "shooting cocaine" is not unknown, nor is the sharing of needles. For teens who become

AIDS—Prevention, Assistance

chemically dependent, prostitution to obtain funds for drugs or the exchange of sex for drugs is not uncommon, such behaviors further placing them at risk of contacting AIDS and spreading AIDS.

AIDS is not spread through casual contact, toilet seats, door knobs, hand shakes or hugging. Family members of people with AIDS have not contracted the disease, even when towels, food, and drinking cups have been shared. The exception is in the case of sexual contact between family members, when one is infected.

PREVENTION

Education is the only known means of preventing the spread of AIDS. In 1987, the United States Surgeon General released a statement that every school, starting in the middle or junior high school years, should teach about how AIDS is transmitted.

Teaching about AIDS is not done best in large groups, such as assemblies with a speaker. If possible teaching about AIDS should be incorporated into existing health courses. What is taught and how it is taught should be developed with input from teachers, administrators and health professionals.

STUDENT/EMPLOYEE ASSISTANCE

The only things that schools can do to assist a student (or employee) with AIDS or the school-age family member of an AIDS victim, is to be knowledgeable about the disease, be prepared to dispel myths about the disease and assist the student (employee) to continue his/her education (career) in an environment as normal as possible.

POLICY ON AIDS

The time to decide how to handle a case of AIDS in the school (student or staff) is before the situation arises. While the number of actual cases of AIDS in school-age children is very low, there are other AIDS-related situations which the school may encounter, such as employees with AIDS or students or employees with family members with AIDS. Policy should be developed, with input from the medical community, administrative and teaching staff, employee associations, parents and health professionals. The policy should be firmly based on facts related to the transmission of the disease and be consistent with state and federal laws and guidelines. The policy can either be a separate AIDS policy or incorporated into existing policies. The policy should cover those in the school community who have AIDS and those who have contact with those who have AIDS. The Centers for Disease Control (CDC), based on medical evidence and the laws, provide the following policy recommendations concerning the education of students with AIDS:

Centers for Disease Control
Recommendations for the Education of
AIDS-Infected Children
August 1985

- Decisions regarding the type of educational and care setting for AIDS-infected children should be based on the behavior, neurologic development and physical condition of the child and the expected type of interaction with others in that setting. These decisions are best made using the team approach, including the child's physician, public health personnel, the child's parent or guardian and personnel associated with the proposed care or educational setting. In each case, risks and benefits to both the infected child and to others in the setting should be weighed.
- For most infected school-age children, the benefits of an unrestricted setting would outweigh the risks of their acquiring potentially harmful infections in the setting and the apparent nonexistent risk of transmission of AIDS. These children should be allowed to attend school and after-school daycare in an unrestricted setting.
- Care involving exposure to the infected child's body fluids and excrement, such as feeding and diaper changing, should be performed by persons who are aware of the child's AIDS infection and the modes of possible transmission. In any setting involving an AIDS-infected person, good handwashing after exposure to blood and body fluids and before caring for another child should be observed, and gloves should be worn if open lesions are present on the caretaker's hands. Any open lesions on the infected person should also be covered.
- Because other infections in addition to AIDS can be present in blood or body fluids, all schools and daycare facilities,

regardless of whether children with AIDS infection are attending, should adopt routine procedures for handling blood or body fluids. Soiled surfaces should be promptly cleaned with disinfectants, such as household bleach (diluted one part bleach to 10 parts water). Disposable towels or tissues should be used whenever possible, and mops should be rinsed in the disinfectant. Those who are cleaning should avoid exposure of open skin lesions or mucous membranes to the blood or body fluids.

- The hygienic practices of children with AIDS infection may improve as the child matures. Alternatively, the hygienic practices may deteriorate if the child's condition worsens. Evaluation to assess the need for a restricted environment should be performed regularly.
- Mandatory screening as a condition for school entry is not warranted based on available data.
- Persons involved in the care and education of AIDS-infected children should respect the child's right to privacy, including maintaining confidential records. The number of personnel who are aware of the child's condition should be kept at the minimum needed to assure proper care of the child and to detect situations where the potential for transmission may increase (e.g., bleeding injury).
- All educational and public health departments, regardless of whether AIDS-infected children are involved, are strongly encouraged to inform parents, children and educators regarding AIDS, and its transmission. Such education would greatly assist efforts to provide the best care and education for infected children while minimizing the risk of transmission to others.

For more information, contact Centers for Disease Control, 1600 Clifton Road, Bldg. 6, Room 277, Atlanta, GA 30333.

Source: Morbidity and Mortality Weekly Report, Aug. 30, 1985

HANDLING AN AIDS-RELATED "CRISIS"

When the school staff and/or community becomes aware that a student or employee has AIDS or even a family member of a student or employee has AIDS, the school can be faced with a highly charged emotional situation.

While the CDC reports that there has never been an identified case of AIDS traced to transmission in school, daycare, or foster-care situations or through the casual person-to-person contact associated with a school type setting, myths about the transfer of the disease still abound. The role of the school is education, including the teaching of facts and the dispelling of myths. Probably at no time is the commitment to education more critical than when the school is faced with an AIDS-related situation. Decisions need to be made based on facts and presented in a credible manner to staff, community, parents and students.

When AIDS was first identified, the few school-age cases were traced to contaminated blood used for transfusions. It is unlikely that schools will encounter new cases of AIDS which have been contracted in this manner.

The new cases of AIDS encountered by the schools will have been contracted either through the sharing of needles for intravenous drug use or through sexual contact. In the case of students, AIDS may be contracted before the age of 18, but the person may not become symptomatic until after graduation. However, these asymptomatic carriers can spread the disease. The school, in these situations may not have to deal directly with a case of AIDS, but may face criticism for not providing adequate educational programs to prevent the spread of the disease.

AIDS can also be spread from an infected mother to her unborn child during pregnancy or birth. Children who contract the disease in this manner usually die before the age of school entry. However, advances in the treatment of AIDS may change this situation.

Probably the most likely AIDS-related situation to be faced by the school is the case of a family member of a student who contracts AIDS. While the student does not have AIDS and cannot spread the disease, myths and fear about the disease may trigger negative emotional responses from parents, community, staff and other students.

If the school is presented with an AIDS-related situation, the following steps are recommended:

– Implement the district policy on AIDS.

Or, if there is no policy:

– Review the Centers for Disease Control (CDC) guidelines. Get good medical advice from physicians familiar with AIDS (for example, call the American Pediatrics Association. Not all doctors are knowledgeable about AIDS), and get advice from the departments of health and education in your state.

- Develop an action plan.
- Keep control, make informed decisions and then don't change your mind.
- Designate a spokesperson.
- Once you have your facts and plan in order, talk to and educate the staff, parents and community.
- Maintain confidentiality of the child or staff member with AIDS.

How it Works—A Case Study
AIDS

The following case study centers on a student who does not have AIDS but who has an older brother who has contracted the disease.

Monday Morning

Mrs. Jones, a guidance counselor at Johnson High School, brings in an article which appeared in the paper of the town fifty miles away where State College is located. The headline on page one reads "State College Football Star Has AIDS." The article goes on to identify the student as a graduate of Johnson High School. While no name is given it is clear from the article that the student is a boy who graduated two years ago from Johnson High School, named Billy Carl. Bob Carl, his younger brother, is currently a junior at Johnson High. Several things are clear to the principal:

- The press will be calling shortly for the school's response to the ex-student with AIDS and questions about how the school is going to deal with his brother currently at Johnson High.
- Staff and students in the school already know or will shortly know about the article and have figured out who the former student is.
- Parents will begin to call concerned about the safety of their children attending school with a boy who has a brother with AIDS.
- The Carl family must be under incredible stress having a son diagnosed as having a fatal disease. In addition, the family is further under stress because of societal fear of the disease, and knowledge and ignorance about how it is contracted.

- Bob, the current Johnson High junior, besides his worry over his brother having a fatal disease, will be subject to additional stress because of fear of AIDS.
- The school's concern is for Bob. What the school does or does not do will have a profound effect on his future.

The principal determines that Bob is absent from school that day. He thanks the counselor for the information and asks who Bob's counselor is. After the counselor leaves he informs his secretary to hold any calls from the press or parents, but to assure callers that he will return their calls. No information concerning current or past students is to be provided by the secretary.

The principal calls the superintendent and explains the situation. A meeting is planned for 10:00 A.M., with the superintendent, president of the Board of Education, school physician, PTA president, chairperson of the Student Assistance Team, director of guidance and the principal.

Monday—8:30 a.m.

The principal calls the Carl home. Mrs. Carl answers the phone. The principal explains that the article in the paper has come to the attention of the school. He expresses empathy for what the family must be experiencing. Mrs. Carl confirms that it has indeed been a nightmare. Not only is she distraught about Billy's disease but also about the effect it is having on Bob. They have received terrible phone calls and Bob says he will not go back to school. The principal assures Mrs. Carl that the school will do everything possible to help Bob through this difficult time.

The principal learns that when Billy was a senior in high school he experimented with cocaine and once attended a party where there was casual sex and he thinks he may have shared a needle with others at the party. The party was attended by a few Johnson High students and some older people who were working or were going to college. Billy didn't know most of them.

Finally, Mrs. Carl tells the principal that all family members were tested for AIDS after Billy's diagnosis and are free from the virus antibodies.

Monday—9:00 a.m.

The principal meets with the Student Assistance Team, Director of Guidance, the nurse, Bob's counselor and the assistant principals. He determines that they have all either seen the article or heard rumors. Some have even heard that the younger brother Bob also has AIDS. He clarifies the situation as he knows it. He reviews the district policy with them, states that all outside requests for information will be directed to him and tells them about the planned 10:00 meeting.

Monday—10:00 a.m.

At the meeting with key administrators and communicators, the principal explains the situation. The policy is reviewed and the following decisions made:

- Bob does not have AIDS and does not pose any health threat to the students or staff.
- Bob will remain in school and no special provisions concerning his program or interactions with staff or students will be initiated.
- The aim of the school will be to maintain normalcy, disseminate facts about the disease as needed and dispel myths.
- Even though the student's name is generally known, the school will not name the student or confirm the name of the student to the press.

The following plan of action is agreed to:

- The principal will act as the official spokesperson: all questions from the press will be directed to him.
- The school physician will call the doctors in town who service the most students (identified by the nurse from student record cards) to prepare them for calls from concerned parents. She will also attend the faculty meeting to answer questions.
- Bob's guidance counselor will call Bob about returning to school and if necessary visit him at home.
- The president of the PTA will contact the other PTA presidents in town and explain the situation. If major parental concern develops, a special meeting will be called by the PTA for parents. Emphasis in communications will be on providing support for the family and the student.
- The president of the board will contact other board members, review policy and the plan of action.
- The superintendent will meet with other principals and administrators in the district to explain in general the situation and plan of action.
- The nurse will be prepared to talk with parents who think their own children may have been exposed to AIDS at the same time Billy was or may even be concerned because of lifestyle activities of their children.

- A large supply of fact sheets on AIDS and the district policy will be printed and available.
- The superintendent and principal will set up a meeting with the Carls, preferably at their home, to review the actions which the school will take (meeting at their home will show by example that school officials will act on fact not on fear).

Monday—12:00 noon

At a meeting with Bob's current teachers, the principal explains the situation and the plan of action. The importance of supporting Bob and not treating him any differently than usual is emphasized. The school nurse or physician answers questions the teachers may have about the disease. The guidance counselor or school psychologist explains some of the problems Bob may face and recommends how the staff might respond. The student's name is shared with his teachers. They are also told that the name will not be used in the faculty meeting nor will the name be confirmed to the press. If parents call any teacher, they should be directed to the principal.

Monday—1:00 p.m.

The superintendent and the principal visit the Carls; both Billy and Bob are there. Billy has been in the hospital but is now home. He plans to return to college in a few days.

The principal explains the actions the school has taken and will take. He recognizes that there may be some negative comments made to Bob when he returns to school but affirms that the school and his teachers will be supportive. Bob says that he has already talked to his guidance counselor and has told him he will come back to school tomorrow.

Monday—2:30 p.m.

The principal, school physician, and superintendent meet with the entire faculty. The situation is reviewed and false rumors put to rest. The district plan concerning the handling of the situation is explained. Copies of the fact sheet on AIDS and the district policy, distributed earlier in the year, are distributed again. The principal reports on the visit to the student's home and the fact that the student will return to school soon and that his brother with AIDS is returning to college. The physician answers any health related questions. The principal and superintendent answer questions related to the school.

Tuesday

Bob returns to school. Teachers report that there have been a few questions in their classes, but they feel that the fact that the students have studied AIDS in health class has minimized student concern. Several parents have called the principal. In most cases their questions were addressed and if they were still concerned it was suggested that they discuss their concerns with their doctor. One parent stated she was transferring her son to a private school.

The local paper carried a front page article concerning the college student with AIDS and mentioning that he had a younger brother in the high school. They reported that the principal provided them with the school policy on AIDS, explained that a student who has a family member with AIDS is not a risk to the school community; nor in fact is a student with AIDS a threat to the school community, except in some very extreme cases as provided for in the policy. However, the principal would not comment on the presence in the school of the brother of the reported AIDS victim nor comment on the reported AIDS victim.

Friday—9:00 a.m.

The principal meets again with the key administrators, PTA president and school physician. They agree that there was a minimum of controversy and educational disruption. A couple of parents did keep their children home from school for a day or two but they have returned. The teachers have reacted sympathetically and professionally. Bob appears to be doing well in school. Some students have been particularly supportive both in and out of school. He has had some problems with some of his previous friends. Their parents don't mind their being friends with Bob in school but do not want their children to see him socially out of school. The guidance counselor has seen Bob several times and his parents have also arranged for outside counseling.

SUMMARY

AIDS is a disease which is a direct concern for every school. It is an incurable fatal disease spread in body fluids during sexual contact or through contact with contaminated blood. AIDS is not spread by casual contact.

Education on prevention of the disease is the only means society now has to control the spread of AIDS. The Surgeon General of the United States recommends that education concerning AIDS prevention be part of the school curriculum.

Schools need to be prepared to constructively handle situations related to students and staff who have AIDS and the non-infected child relatives of AIDS victims. Policy and plans for coping with AIDS-related problems should be formulated and be based on law, medical facts, rights of privacy and the needs of students and staff.

CHAPTER 9

Anorexia and Bulimia

THE PROBLEM

Our society has traditionally been weight conscious. It is estimated that 90 percent of all female teenagers are dissatisfied with
their weight.

Virtually all of these dissatisfied teenagers have tried one or
more diets, frequently switching from one fad diet to another.

Approximately 20–30 percent of the high school female population will experience complications serious enough to affect their
health as a result of trying to modify their body shape and weight.

A Gallup Poll found that one in five teenagers has used drastic
means such as self-induced vomiting or diuretics to control weight
(reported in Sandt, 1986).

By college age, approximately 19 percent of the students, most of
them females, have developed the eating disorder characterized by
binge eating followed by self-induced purging. The disorder may
last as long as twenty years and be marked by increasingly frequent binge-purge episodes (Harris, 1983).

Hundreds of thousands of young people have anorexia nervosa, a
potentially fatal disorder (Scriptographic Booklet, 1986).

It is estimated that between 5–20 percent of those with anorexia
or bulimia will die of complications of the diseases, including
suicide (Horne, 1980).

WHAT ARE ANOREXIA AND BULIMIA?

Anorexia nervosa and bulimia are both eating disorders. The
American Psychiatric Association defines anorexia as the loss of 25
percent of appropriate body weight. Bulimia refers to the secret
pattern of binge eating and self-induced vomiting and abuse of
cathartic or diuretic drugs, resulting in fluctuation of body weight

141

(*Diagnostic and Statistical Manual of Mental Disorders,* third edition, 1980).

WHO DEVELOPS AN EATING DISORDER?

Anorexia nervosa and bulimia are disorders which usually appear in people between the ages of 13 and 25, with many more girls developing the disorder than boys. The typical teenager who develops an eating disorder is from a middle to upper middle class family and is often described as a "model" child. He/she is frequently heavily involved with his/her parents and tries to live up to what is perceived as the family's expectations. One theory is that the eating disorder occurs when the child's coping and defense skills are overwhelmed at the time of maturation leading to insecurity and self-doubt (Crisp, 1980). In the case of anorexia, dieting becomes a means of taking charge of the person's own life by attempting to perfect appearance. Preoccupation with food and weight may also be a means for avoiding growing up and dealing with problems. Thus, food becomes the enemy to be overcome. In the case of bulimia, the person lacks impulse-control and turns to food as a means to relieve anxiety-provoking situations. Overeating is followed by feelings of guilt and then purging behavior. The binge-purge cycle eventually dominates the person's life, leaving little time for school or social relationships.

THE SYMPTOMS OF ANOREXIA NERVOSA

- Excessive weight loss, often covered by wearing layers of baggy clothing
- Avoidance of eating, doing homework or other activities during lunch, being too busy to eat dinner or breakfast
- Absence of menstruation
- Perfectionism
- Considering him-/herself too fat
- Preoccupation with food and dieting
- Sensitivity to cold
- Heavy involvement with physical activities
- Unusual eating habits, such as eating tiny bites of food, long list of disliked foods

— Denial that there is a problem
— Withdrawal from social activities

THE SYMPTOMS OF BULIMIA

— Near normal weight but the tendency for weight to fluctuate
— Perfectionism
— Abuse of laxatives and diuretics with many visits to the bathroom necessary
— Preoccupation with food
— Dieting and exercise
— Changes in appearance such as skin rashes, swollen salivary glands
— Alcohol and drug abuse for some
— Depression and isolation
— Secretive behavior which may include stealing of many foods and laxatives
— Frequent mood swings
— Abnormal tooth decay and gum damage
— Drop in grades
— Frequent complaints of nausea, sore throat, headaches, cramps, tiredness and weakness
— Lack of ability to concentrate
— Many absences from school
— Sudden drop in weight between football and wrestling seasons

THE SCHOOL'S ROLE IN ASSISTING STUDENTS WITH EATING DISORDERS

Information on eating disorders should be part of the health curriculum. Included in the program should be discussions concerning the role of society in setting the implied standards for appearance, normal growth patterns, nutrition and constructive means for dealing with anxiety.

Once the pattern of an eating disorder has been established, it is the role of school personnel to assist in the identification of the disease and assist the student and his/her parents to get treatment.

Getting assistance for the student with anorexia nervosa or bulimia is not usually easy. Just as in drug/alcohol abuse there is heavy denial on the part of the student. In the case of anorexia the severe weight loss may make the need for treatment obvious to parents and school staff. In the case of bulimia, the student may appear at near normal weight and excuses for unusual or secretive behavior may seem more plausible. Therefore, with eating disorders it is likely that either the school staff, parents or a combination of both will have to use confrontation to break through denial and get the student to recognize the need for help. The form included in the chapter on Student Assistance (pages 79–82) can be used to collect data and the process for confrontation in the chapter on Drugs/Alcohol can be adapted for overcoming denial.

How it Works—A Case Study
Bulimia

Following is a case study which illustrates how the school staff can identify a potential eating disorder and guide a student to assistance.

Tuesday Afternoon

A student is sent by the cheerleading coach to get the school nurse. Sandra, a cheerleader, has passed out during practice. In the few minutes it takes the nurse to get to the gym, Sandra has come to and is sitting up. She says that she feels fine and is getting a cold and has a sore throat. Her pulse is slightly low, but otherwise she seems fine. The nurse accompanies Sandra to the nurse's office, where, on brief examination, she notes that Sandra seems to have enlarged parotid glands.

The nurse calls Sandra's mother to explain what has happened and suggest that she take Sandra to the doctor for an examination. Mrs. Smith, Sandra's mother, is concerned: there was another time recently when her daughter felt faint. She will call the doctor and pick Sandra up.

While they are waiting for Mrs. Smith, the nurse reviews Sandra's health file. Sandra has come to the nurse's office several times in the last two months. The complaint has been a sore throat and Sandra has requested to be excused from physical education. The nurse considers that Sandra might be suffering from bulimia and asks her if she is ever sick to her stomach. Sandra quickly denies any problem. Mrs. Smith arrives and takes Sandra to the doctor.

Wednesday Morning

Mrs. Smith calls to say the doctor thinks that Sandra has been doing too much and is coming down with a cold. He wants her to stay home and rest for a day or two.

Wednesday Team Meeting

The nurse discusses Sandra with the team. She is still concerned that Sandra's problem may be more serious than a cold. The team decides to collect data.

Friday Team Meeting

The nurse reports:
- Sandra's physical education teacher reports that she has had a series of "excuses" to avoid taking gym and has been warned by the teacher that if the behavior continues, she will fail and not be allowed to continue as a cheerleader.
- Sandra's English teacher reports that she has been late coming from lunch to class a number of times recently. Her excuse is that she had to go to the girls' room. Sandra has always been a solid "B" student but her grades are dropping into the "C" range.
- The assistant principal reports that for the first time in the three years that Sandra has been in the school, she was sent to the office for disciplinary action. A teacher on hall duty had found her in the girls' room without a pass and at a time she should have been in class.
- The cheerleading coach reports that Sandra seems to have lost some of her enthusiasm. She attends practice but participates only to the minimal degree required. She seems to be less involved with the other cheerleaders.

The team decides the nurse should meet with Mrs. Smith and share the information.

Meeting with Mrs. Smith

The nurse meets with Mrs. Smith and shares the findings of the team. She explains that the information suggests that Sandra may have an eating disorder. Mrs. Smith says that she and her husband have been concerned about Sandra and maybe the school staff is right. She tells the nurse that only the week before, she had found an empty can of cake frosting in the garbage. She had accused Sandra's little brother and his friend but they had denied eating it.

She now believes that perhaps Sandra had been the culprit. Mrs. Smith also remembered finding a package of laxatives in Sandra's room.

Mrs. Smith and the nurse decide to confront Sandra with the information. Sandra at first denies that there is any problem. However, after listening to all the information she admits that she has been taking laxatives to control her weight and occasionally gets sick to her stomach after lunch. When pressed for how often this occurs, she finally admits that it is almost every day. She also admits that recently she hasn't been able to control the urge to vomit after eating. But she says that she certainly isn't starving to death. She may not always eat the right foods, but for example she ate a huge dish of ice cream the night before. The nurse asks if it was just a dish. Mrs. Smith says, "I bought a half gallon of ice cream yesterday for tonight's supper and it was all gone this morning." Sandra admits that she did eat all of it.

The nurse asks Sandra if she remembers studying bulimia in health class. Sandra says she does remember, and maybe she is a little like the case they studied. Mrs. Smith asks what they can do. The nurse suggests that they see a doctor who specializes in eating disorders. The nurse gives Mrs. Smith a list of doctors in the area.

Call From Mrs. Smith

Mrs. Smith calls the nurse during the next week to tell her that the doctor has confirmed that Sandra has bulimia and she is receiving outpatient treatment. Mrs. Smith thanks the nurse for being so alert to a problem.

Team Meeting

The nurse reports to the team that Sandra is receiving treatment. The team makes a note to do a follow-up with Sandra's teachers in two months.

THE TREATMENT FOR EATING DISORDERS

Treatment of eating disorders usually combines several approaches, including:
— medical treatment
— individual psychotherapy
— family counseling

- behavior modification training
- education concerning the disease and nutrition
- group therapy

Depending on the severity of the case and the existence or non-existence of other medical problems related to the disease, the student may be hospitalized or treated as an outpatient. If the person is hospitalized for a period of time, outpatient treatment is continued upon release from the hospital. Treatment for the disease is usually long-term and relapses frequently occur.

SUMMARY

Anorexia nervosa and bulimia are eating disorders which usually begin in adolescence. If left untreated, these eating disorders can become debilitating and life threatening. The earlier the problem is diagnosed the more likely it is to be controlled. The school can play a significant role in assisting students with eating disorders by including study of the disorders in the curriculum, teaching staff to recognize the symptoms and developing a means for collecting information concerning student behaviors and using that information to get medical assistance.

CHAPTER 10

Teen Pregnancy

THE PROBLEM

U.S. teens under the age of 15 are at least 15 times more likely to give birth than their peers in any other western nation. More than one million teenage girls in the United States become pregnant every year. Approximately 40 percent of these pregnancies end in abortions. As unbelievable as it may seem, teen births now comprise almost one-eighth of all births recorded in the United States (March of Dimes, 1986). One in four girls becomes pregnant before leaving school (National Research Council, 1987).

The proportion of babies born to unwed teenagers has increased at an alarming rate. In 1983, 54 percent of the nearly half million babies born to teenagers were children of unwed mothers compared to 5 percent in 1960 (Select Committee on Children, Youth and Families, 1987). Eight out of ten teenage pregnancies are unintended (National Research Center, 1987).

Although the number of teen pregnancies has not substantially increased since the mid 70's, the problem continues to be a significant social, health, economic and, in many respects, a school issue:

- Two out of three pregnant teens drop out of school.
- With her education cut short, the teenage mother may lack sufficient skills to maintain a self-sufficient lifestyle and, thus, may become dependent on government assistance.
- Teenage marriages have a great chance to end in divorce.
- Families headed by young mothers are seven times more likely to live in poverty.
- Almost one-half of all pregnant teenagers do not receive first trimester prenatal care; pregnant teenagers are almost three times more likely as older mothers to receive late or no prenatal care.
- Babies born to teenagers often are born too small, too soon,

thus having a higher risk of serious health and future learning problems.

THE SCHOOL'S ROLE IN PREGNANCY PREVENTION

Curriculum

It would seem most appropriate that schools provide programs specifically aimed at educating students to the social, health and economic risks related to sex and teen pregnancies. Sex education, in one form or another, is now a common part of the school curriculum. These programs vary greatly in their focus. Common features include information on the psychological and interpersonal aspects of sexuality and specific instruction aimed at promoting rational and informed decision making. Nevertheless, only 40 percent of sex education classes have as their goal the prevention of pregnancy (Kenney & Orr, 1984).

Despite the inevitable attacks by individuals or groups within the community, sex education classes are probably the most widely accepted mechanisms schools have to deal with the issue of adolescent sexuality. Unfortunately, because of ill-defined objectives, there is little to suggest that these programs do, in fact, reduce the risk of teenage pregnancies (Murasksin, 1986).

School professionals must become increasingly familiar with the facts as they relate to sex education. To make these programs successful, careful assessment must first be made as to program goals. In addition, schools must be sensitive to their communities so that there is a greater understanding of the role of the school as it attempts to meet the needs and expectations of the people it serves.

Sex education curricula have not substantially changed over the past 20 to 25 years (Kenney, 1984). The most significant new sex education curriculum was introduced in 1983 by The Center for Population Options (CPO) in Washington, D.C. This program, "Life Planning Education," differs from traditional sex education approaches. It provides instruction on everything from personal growth to resume writing. It approaches sex education from a practical angle, teaching the effects of pregnancy on education, career and earning power. It is designed to be politically acceptable to communities that reject a more straightforward approach (Center for Population Options, 1983).

As with most other sex education programs, little evidence exists to substantiate the effect of the CPO program on sexual behavior or teen pregnancy rates. Yet, it provides a vehicle by which schools can expand the scope of their sex education offering to provide a more interdisciplinary approach to adolescent problems.

Studies also show that general academic success is associated with a reduction in pregnancy rates. Girls under the age of 16 with poor basic skills are five times more likely to become pregnant than girls with average skills. Boys with a low level of basic skills are three times more likely to become teenage fathers (Children's Defense Fund, 1986). Therefore, programs simply directed at improving basic skills may indirectly also be counted as pregnancy prevention programs.

School-Based or School-Linked Clinics

Amidst a rise of controversy, over one hundred in-school clinics aimed at improving adolescent health and preventing unwanted pregnancies have been established (Center for Population Options, 1986). These centers are primarily located in urban schools where there is less likelihood for students to have access to counseling and/or a personal physician. Some clinics dispense contraceptives, some merely provide counseling and referrals. Another approach is the establishment of school-linked clinics. These clinics are outside of the school but are designed to work with the school. A study of one such program in Baltimore showed a 30 percent decrease in teenage pregnancy in the associated schools (Zabin, 1986).

The social, moral and religious issues associated with these bold approaches to address teen pregnancy have caused great controversy. It is not the authors' intent to promote or discourage the implementation of school-based clinic programs. Instead, it is critical that schools and communities carefully survey the nature of teen pregnancies in their community and develop curricula/programs that are tailored to meet the unique needs of the community to be served.

THE SCHOOL'S ROLE IN EDUCATING AND ASSISTING PREGNANT TEENAGERS

Unwanted teen pregnancy is a reality which school professionals must face. Despite the assumption that pregnancy is a family or, at best, a social service issue, school personnel are often knowledgeable about pregnancies in the school. Thus, school curricula, pamphlets in the nurse's and guidance offices, etc., must address the health issues related to pregnancies. Specifically, expecting mothers need to know more about the health risks that poor nutrition, smoking, drinking alcohol and taking drugs have on an unborn baby.

Schools also have a long-range reason for providing assistance to pregnant students. Within five to six years of the birth of the babies, these children of children will enter school. Negative factors which affect the children prenatally or in early life will influence how well the children will do in school and their needs for special school services. A study by the National Research Council (1987) found that for each additional year of school completed by the teenage mothers, the likelihood of their children having to repeat a grade was reduced by 50 percent.

Consistent with the theme of this book, if any member of the school staff becomes aware of a situation that affects the health or well-being of a student, direct intervention with the student and parents should take place. As previously stated, students within the school should have previous knowledge of this ongoing, working policy. In this way, the school personnel (or Student Assistance Team) can work cooperatively with the student and her parents in dealing with this very sensitive, emotional issue. It is our belief that only through this cooperative relationship can the child avoid the agonizing emotional and real physical dangers associated with unwanted pregnancies.

School officials should be prepared to provide the family with a list of counseling and medical agencies that will help the family through difficult times and decisions. Further, a member of the Student Assistance Team, school nurse, guidance counselor, or other concerned staff member should maintain contact with the child and her family. This linkage of educational, social and medical agencies provides ongoing support for the student and her family.

EDUCATING THE PREGNANT TEENAGER

Alternative Educational Programs

One approach used by schools is to provide an alternative educational program for pregnant students. These programs are usually provided in a separate facility near the school. In addition to the regular academic studies the students receive special instruction related to child bearing and parenting. Emphasis is also placed on making realistic plans for support of mother and child and in preventing future unintended pregnancies.

In some cases the total school program is conducted in the alternative facility; in other cases students are mainstreamed for some subjects in the regular high school.

There is evidence to support the belief that effective alternative programs for pregnant students can reduce dropout rate, reduce the number of subsequent unintended pregnancies, improve the health of the mother and increase baby birth weight to levels associated with good health and unimpaired learning potential (Programs That Work, Educational Services for School-age Parents, 1986.)

Mainstream Programs

Societal attitudes toward pregnant teens have changed drastically over the past few years. Previously, a great deal of overt or covert hostility was directed toward pregnant adolescents. Currently, there is a marked trend toward and acceptance for mainstreaming pregnant and parenting teens with the rest of the school population (Weiner, 1987). Further, of the 716 school officials responding to the Educational Research Group Study, 62 percent said mainstreaming has no effect on other teens, and 25 percent said mainstreaming discourages other teens from becoming pregnant.

When asked what services they thought were most effective for pregnant teens and teen parents, respondents to one study ranked personal counseling first, followed by intensive parenting education and family planning, referrals, child care, and alternative schools. Of the respondents' own districts, 78.2 percent provided personal counseling, 53.6 percent provided referrals to local agencies, 22.2 percent provided alternative schools, 19.6 percent provided intensive parenting education and family planning, and 10.6 percent provided child care (Weiner, 1987).

Many find the trend of mainstreaming "very encouraging," since despite the warm and supportive environments of alternative facilities for pregnant teens, these facilities may provide less academically significant programs.

How it Works—A Case Study
Pregnancy

Student Assistance Team Meeting

The physical education teacher has submitted a Student Referral Form to the Student Assistance Team. Carol, a junior student, has the appearance of being pregnant. In the past the student has been very active in sports and in gym class. Recently, she has been presenting excuses for not changing for class. The teacher has overheard two girls say that Carol is pregnant. Carol also appears depressed and yesterday she started to cry at the end of class. The teacher asked her if anything was wrong, but Carol denied having any problems.

The team decides to ask Carol's teachers to complete a referral form; the nurse, guidance counselor and administrator on the team will check their records.

Student Assistance Team Meeting Three Days Later

The teachers report significant changes in the student's behavior in the past three months. Never a very good student, Carol is now in danger of failing two courses. The nurse reports that Carol has been sick to her stomach and has come to the nurse's office twice in the past few weeks. The team decides to have Carol's guidance counselor discuss the information and the staff's concern with Carol.

Meeting with Carol

The guidance counselor schedules a meeting with Carol. At the meeting, she explains to Carol that she and Carol's teachers are concerned. She also explains that while she wants to have an open discussion with Carol, if Carol tells her anything which would seriously affect her health or safety she would not be able to keep it in confidence. Therefore, Carol need not answer any questions she might ask. Carol says that she understands and the counselor presents the information the team has gathered and asks Carol if she is pregnant. Carol breaks down and cries. She is very scared. Although her boyfriend wants her to have an abortion, she thinks abortion is wrong. Moreover, she is afraid to tell her parents. She got pregnant one night after a party where she and her boyfriend were drinking heavily. She has continued to "drink a little" in order to forget her problems. However, it isn't working. It is becoming obvious that she is pregnant and her parents are going to notice. She doen't know what she should do.

The counselor asks Carol if she would like to call her mother and have her come to school and have the counselor there when she tells her mother. Carol readily agrees.

Meeting with the Mother

The counselor and Carol meet with the mother and Carol tells her that she is pregnant. Carol's drinking is also discussed. The mother is shocked and upset, but after some time begins to accept the information and focus on what to do next. They decide to tell Carol's father that night and discuss the options. The counselor gives the mother the name of a clinic which has services to support teenagers while they are pregnant and has an alcohol treatment program. Carol will meet with the counselor in the morning.

Student Assistance Team Meeting Several Days Later

The counselor reports to the team that indeed Carol is pregnant and is planning to have the baby. Arrangements are made for the nurse to meet regularly with Carol to insure that she is getting prenatal medical care and to discuss nutrition. She will continue to meet with the counselor to discuss school work and for career planning. Carol will receive tutoring from a student in the Student Tutoring program. Carol has told the counselor that she is going for outpatient treatment for what has turned out to be a significant drinking problem. The baby's father, a student in another school, has no resources and wants nothing to do with Carol or the baby. The activities and services provided by the school have the following aims:

- keep Carol in school and passing
- get treatment for the alcohol problem
- support Carol in seeking adequate medical attention and getting proper nutrition so that she will have a healthy baby
- assist Carol in making realistic plans for supporting the baby and herself

SUMMARY

Teen pregnancy will affect one out of every four girls before they leave school. Strategies to prevent unintended pregnancies include sex education, development of life skills, basic skills improvement programs, and career planning.

Once teens become pregnant, counseling and support services are needed. The aims of the school's support services are to have the expectant mother and father remain in school and graduate, to develop and implement realistic career plans and to provide information concerning the importance and availability of prenatal and child care.

Appendix A

The following agencies provide a wide variety of publications, services and information concerning the risks to learning covered in this book. Many of these agencies can assist schools to contact local services available in the immediate area of the school.

ALCOHOL AND DRUGS

Al-Anon Family Groups, Box 182, Madison Square Station, New York, NY 10159-0182. (212) 683-1771.

Alcohol, Drug Abuse and Mental Health Administration (ADAMHA), 5600 Fishers Lane, Rockville, MD 20857. (301) 443-4797.

Alcoholics Anonymous, P.O. Box 459, Grand Central Station, New York, NY 10163. (212) 686-1100.

Educational Services District #121, "Here's Looking At You, 2000," Seattle, Washington.

Families Anonymous, 14617 Victory, #1, Van Nuys, CA 91411. (818) 989-7841.

Mothers Against Drunk Driving (MADD), 669 Airport Freeway, Suite 310, Hurst, Texas 76053. (817) 268-6232.

Narcotics Education, Inc., 6830 Laurel St., N.W., Washington, DC 20012. (800) 548-8700.

National Association for Children of Alcoholics, 31706 Coast Highway, Suite 201, South Laguna, CA 92677. (714) 499-3889.

National Cocaine Hotline, 1-800-COCAINE.

National Council on Alcoholism, 12 West 21st Street, 7th Floor, New York, NY 10010. (212) 206-6770.

National Federation of Parents for Drug-Free Youth, 1820 Franwell Ave., Suite 16, Silver Springs, MD 20902. (301) 649-7100.

157

National Institute of Alcohol Abuse and Alcoholism (NIAAA), P.O. Box 2345, Rockville, MD 20852. (301) 468-2600 (US Clearinghouse).

National Institute on Drug Abuse (NIDA), Room 10-A-43, 5600 Fisher Lane, Rockville, MD 20852. (301) 443-6500 (US Clearinghouse).

National PTA Alcohol Educations Publications, 700 North Rush St., Chicago, IL 60611. (312) 787-0977.

Parent Resources Institute for Drug Education (PRIDE) and Student Resource Institute for Drug Education (STRIDE), 100 Edgewood Ave., Suite 1216, Atlanta, GA 30303. (800) 241-9726.

Target, National Federation of State High School Associations, 11724 Plaza Circle, P.O. Box 20626, Kansas City, MO 64195. (816) 464-5400.

Toughlove, P.O. Box 1069, Doylestown, PA 18901. (215) 348-7090.

SUICIDE PREVENTION

National Education Association, Human and Civil Rights, 1201 16th St. N.W., Washington, DC 20036. (202) 833-4000.

National Institute of Mental Health, 1021 Prince St., Alexandria, Virginia 22314.

Youth Suicide National Center, 1825 Eye St., N.W., Suite 400, Washington, DC 20006. (202) 429-0190.

ANOREXIA NERVOSA AND BULIMIA

American Anorexia/Bulimia Association, Inc., 133 Cedar Lane, Teaneck, NJ 07666. (201) 836-1800.

Anorexia Nervosa and Related Eating Disorders, Inc., P.O. Box 5102, Eugene, OR 97405. (503) 344-1144.

Center for the Study of Anorexia and Bulimia, 1 West 91st St., New York, NY 10024. (212) 595-3449.

National Anorexia Aid Society, Inc., P.O. Box 23461, Columbus, OH 43229. (614) 895-2009.

National Association of Anorexia Nervosa and Associated Disorders, Inc., (ANAD), P.O. Box 271, Highland Park, IL 60035. (312) 831-3438.

CHILD ABUSE

American Federation of Teachers, AFL-CIO, 555 New Jersey Ave. NW, Washington, DC 20001. (202) 879-4847.

Child Assault Prevention Program, P.O. Box 02084, Columbus, OH 43202. (614) 291-2540.

The National Center for Missing and Exploited Children, 1835 K. St. NW, Suite 700, Washington, DC 20006. (202) 634-3821.

National Center on Child Abuse and Neglect, Children's Bureau, Administration for Children, Youth and Families, US Department of Health and Human Services, P.O. Box 1182, Washington, DC 20013. (202) 245-2840.

National Clearinghouse on Child Abuse and Neglect Information, (301) 251-5157.

National Council on Child Abuse and Family Violence, Washington Square, 1050 Conn. Ave. NW, Washington, DC 20036. (202) 429-6695.

National Education Association, 1201 16th St. NW, Washington, DC 20036. (202) 833-4000.

National PTA, 700 N. Rush St., Chicago, IL 60611. (312) 787-0977.

National Runaway Switchboard, 1-800-621-4000

Runaway Hotline, 1-800-231-6946.

AIDS

AIDS Action Council/Federation of AIDS-related Organizations, 729 8th St. SE, #200, Washington, DC 20003. (202) 547-3101.

AIDS Education Fund, 2335 18th St. NW, Washington, DC 20009. (202) 332-5939.

American Academy of Pediatrics, Office of Government Liaison, 1331 Pennsylvania Ave. NW, Suite 721 North, Washington, DC 20004. (202) 662-7460.

American Council of Life Insurance, Health Insurance Association of America, "Teens and AIDS: Playing It Safe," available in packages of 100, $10.00, Department 190, ACLI/HIAA, 1001 Pennsylvania Ave., NW, Washington, DC 20004-2599.

American Federation of Teachers, 555 New Jersey Ave. NW, Washington, DC 20001. (202) 879-4400.

American Foundation for AIDS Research, 9601 Wilshire Blvd., Mezzanine, Los Angeles, CA 90210. (213) 273-5547.

Centers for Disease Control, 1600 Clifton Rd., Bldg. 6, Room 277, Atlanta, GA 30333. (404) 329-3472.

Lambda Legal Defense and Education Fund, 132 W. 43rd St., New York, NY 10036. (212) 944-9488.

National Association of Independent Schools, 18 Tremont St., Boston, MA 02108. (617) 723-6900.

National Coalition of Gay and Sexually Transmitted Disease Services, P.O. Box 239, Milwaukee, Wis. 53201. (414) 277-7671.

National Education Association, 1201 16th St. NW, Washington, DC 20036. (202) 833-4000.

TEEN PREGNANCY

Alan Guttmacher Institute, 2010 Massachusetts Ave. NW, Suite 500, Washington, DC 20036. (202) 296-4012.

Center for Population Options, 1012 14th St. NW, Suite 1200, Washington, DC 20005. (202) 347-5700.

Children's Defense Fund, 122 C. St. NW, Suite 400, Washington, DC 20001. (202) 628-8787.

Planned Parenthood of America, 810 7th Ave., New York, NY 10019. (212) 541-7800.

Appendix B

EDUCATIONAL PROGRAMS THAT WORK

The following programs have been termed exemplary by the United States Department of Education's Joint Dissemination Review Panel (JDRP), based on objective evidence of effectiveness. The listed programs were selected as resources because they provide materials and demonstrations of proven practices for students at risk. Many of the programs have multiple demonstration sites throughout the country and offer assistance and training to schools wishing to adopt their programs.

FOCUS DISSEMINATION PROJECT–A secondary program for training teachers to provide alternative education for students who are disaffected. Contact: Focus Dissemination Project; Human Resource Associates, Inc., P.O. Box 303, Hastings, MN 55033. (612) 437-3976.

INTERCEPT: A POSITIVE ALTERNATIVE TO PUPIL SUSPENSIONS, TRUANCY AND DROPOUTS–A secondary program which trains teachers in effective discipline procedures, classroom management skills and instructional skills. Contact: Anne M. Dorner Middle School; Van Cortlandt Ave., Ossining, NY. (914) 762-5740.

EDUCATIONAL SERVICES FOR SCHOOL-AGE PARENTS (ESSP)–A program which provides mainstreaming of regular academic subjects, a five-credit course in childcare and development, nutritional training, group and individual counseling and introduction to local service agencies for expectant school-age students. Contact: New Brunswick High School, 1125 Livingston Ave., New Brunswick, NJ 08901. (201) 745-5334.

COOPERATIVE FEDERATION FOR EDUCATIONAL EXPERIENCES (PROJECT COFFEE)–An alternative occupational program in high technology for use with alienated/disaffected secondary students. Contact: Oxford High School Annex, Main Street, Oxford, MA 01540; (617) 987-1626.

INDIVIDUAL PROGRESS PROGRAM–An academic program for gifted students in grades 2–5. The program accelerates students through a basic core curriculum commensurate with the students' ability. Contact: Educational Service District No. 21, 1410 South 200th St., Seattle, WA 98148. (206) 248-4961.

161

ETHICAL ISSUES IN DECISION MAKING—A program which uses a theory of cognitive moral development to foster the moral growth of high school students in school governance and in ethical issues courses. Contact: Scarsdale Public Schools, 45 Wayside Ln., Scarsdale, NY 10583. (914) 723-5500.

INSTITUTE FOR CREATIVE EDUCATION (ICE)—A sequentially ordered curriculum that teaches a creative problem-solving process in many subject areas to heterogeneously grouped and gifted and talented classes, grades K-12. Contact: Educational Information and Resource Center, Box 209, Route 4, Delsea Dr., Sewell, NJ 08080. (609) 228-6000.

SAGE—A program designed to develop higher order and critical thinking skills and higher achievement by providing a differentiated curriculum for gifted and talented elementary students. Contact: Barbieri School, Framingham Public Schools, Dudley Rd., Framingham, MA 01701. (617) 872-4253.

TALENTS UNLIMITED—A structured program which applies a multiple-talent theory to instruction in the regular classroom. Contact: Talents Unlimited, 1107 Arlington St., Mobile, AL 36605. (205) 690-8060.

CAMBRIDGE AND SOMERVILLE PROGRAM FOR ALCOHOL REHABILITATION (CASPER). The Decisions About Drinking curriculum has units for grades 3–12 designed to improve attitudes and cognitive knowledge related to alcohol and alcoholism. Contact: CASPER, 226 Highland Ave., Somerville, MA 02143. (617) 623-2080.

PROJECT CHOICE—A cancer prevention program for grades K–12 designed to reduce the risk of cancer. Contact: Fred Hutchinson Cancer Research Center, 1124 Columbia St., Seattle, WA 98104. (206) 467-4679.

GROWING HEALTHY—A comprehensive K–7 health education program designed to foster student competencies to make decisions enhancing their health and lives. Contact: School Health Program, National Center for Health Education, 2190 Meridan Park Blvd., Suite G, Concord, CA 94520. (415) 676-2813.

THE ME-ME DRUG PREVENTION PROGRAM—A drug prevention program designed to improve self-concept and reduce the likelihood that students will use drugs. Contact: ME-ME Inc., 426 W. College Ave., Appleton, WI 54911. (414) 735-0114.

OMBUDSMAN—A school-based semester-long course designed to reduce psychological and attitudinal states associated with drug use, for use in grades 7–8. Contact: Charlotte Drug Education Center, 1416 E. Morehead, Charlotte, NC 28204. (704) 336-3211.

CURRICULUM FOR MEETING MODERN PROBLEMS (THE NEW MODEL ME)—A curriculum to assist students in grades 9–12 understand the causes and consequences of behavior. The program can be used as a course or to supplement existing courses. Contact: Learning for Life/MSH, Dept. NDN. 165 Allendale Rd., Boston, MA 02130. (617) 524-7799.

LEARNCYCLE—Responsive Teaching. An intensive teacher training program designed to develop flexible, effective skills for managing and teaching mainstreamed or high-risk students. Contact: Highland Public Schools, Washington State Facilitator, 15675 Ambaum Blvd., S.W., Seattle, WA 98166. (206) 433-2453.

ALL CHILDREN TOTALLY INVOLVED IN EXERCISE (ACTIVE)—A diagnostic/prescriptive physical education program that provides teachers with curriculum, skills, strategies, and attitudes necessary to implement a program for handicapped and normal individuals. Contact: Kelso School District #453, Kelso, WA 98626. (206) 577-2410.

NORTHWEST SPECIAL EDUCATION (NWSE)—A program which provides training for classroom teachers so they can effectively focus on specific learning disability students. Contact: Northwest Special Education, R.R. #1, Columbus, ND 58727. (701) 939-6501

Bibliography

Adams, Raymond S. and Bruce J. Biddle. *Realities of Teaching: Explorations With Video Tape,* New York:Holt, Rinehart and Winston.

American Psychiatric Association. *Diagnostic and Statistical Manual of Mental Disorders,* 3rd edition (1980).

Bolton, Iris. "Educated Suicide Prevention," *School Safety* (Spring, 1986).

Brookover, W. B. and L. W. Lezotte. "Changes in School Characteristics Coincident with Change in Student Achievement," (executive summary), Lansing, Mich.:College of Urban Development of Michigan State University and the Michigan Department of Education (1977).

Brophy, J. and T. Good. "Teacher Behaviors and Student Achievement," in Wittrock, ed. *Handbook of Research on Teaching* (3rd Edition), New York:McMillan Publishing Co. (1985).

Brophy, J. E. "Teacher Praise: A Functional Analysis," *Review of Education Research,* Vol. 51, pp. 5–32, (1981).

Bruce, Matthew H. "Establishing Pre-Instructional Set," in Miller, ed. *Skill Building Series: Inter Teaching Program,* Temple University (1976).

Center for Population Options, "Life Planning Education: A Strategy for Teenage Pregnancy Prevention," Washington, D.C. (1986).

Center for Population Options, "School-Based Clinics: Policy Initiatives Around the Country, 1985," Washington, D.C. (January 1986).

Crisp, A. H. *Anorexia Nervosa: Let Me Be,* New York:Grune and Stratton (1980).

Cummings, C., Nelson and Shaw. *Teaching Makes a Difference,* Teaching, Inc. (1980).

Cummings, Carol. *Managing to Teach,* Teaching, Inc. (1983).

Dunn, Rita and Ken Dunn. *Teaching Students Through Their Individual Learning Styles: A Practical Approach,* Reston, Va.:Reston Publishing Co. (1978).

Edmonds, R. R. "A Discussion of the Literature and Issues Related to Effective Schooling," Paper prepared for National Conference on Urban Education, CEMREL, St. Louis, Mo. (July, 1978).

Educational Service District #121. "Here's Looking At You, 2000," Seattle, Washington, Revised (1986).

Emmer, E. and C. Everston. "Effective Management at the Beginning of the School Year in Junior High Classrooms," R & D Center for Teaching Education, University of Texas at Austin (1980).

Everston, Carolyn. "Differences in Instructional Activities in High and Low Achieving Junior High Classes," Research & Development Center for Teacher Education, University of Texas at Austin (March 1980).

Fead, A. Kelley. *The Child Abuse Crisis: Impact on the Schools,* Arlington, Virginia:Capitol Publications (1985).

Gold, Mark. *The Facts About Drugs and Alcohol,* New York:Bantam Books (1986).

Good, T. L. "How Teachers' Expectations Affect Results," *American Education,* 18(10):25–32 (December, 1982).

Good, T. L. and J. E. Brophy. *Looking Into Classrooms,* 3rd Edition, New York:Harper and Row (1984).

Goodlad, J. *A Place Called School,* New York:McGraw-Hill Book Company (1984).

Harris, Robert T. "Bulemorexia and Related Serious Eating Disorders with Medical Complications," *Annals of Internal Medicine,* American College of Physicians, (1983).

Hasazi, Susan, Paul Rice and Robert York. *Mainstreaming: Merging Regular and Special Education,* Bloomington, Indiana:Phi Delta Kappa Education Foundation (1979).

Henley, Martin. *Teaching Mildly Retarded Children in the Regular Classroom,* Bloomington, Indiana:Phi Delta Kappa Educational Foundation (1985).

Highland Park School District, Michigan. "HIT: High Intensity Tutoring," in *Educational Programs That Work,* 7th edition, United States Department of Education (Fall, 1980).

Hoffman, L. "Early Childhood Experiences and Women's Achievement Motives," *Journal of Social Issues,* 28:129–155 (1972).

Horne, Robert. "Anorexia Nervosa," *Carrier Foundation Letter,* Bell Mead, N.J., 58 (January 1980).

Horton, Lowell. "Adolescent Alcohol Abuse," Fastback 217, Bloomington, Indiana:Phi Delta Kappa Education Foundation (1985).

"House Select Committee on Children, Youth and Families," Report, Washington, D.C. (1987).

Hunter, Madeline. *Reinforcement Theory for Teachers,* El Segundo, California:TIP Publications (1985).

Hunter, Madeline. *Retention Theory for Teachers,* El Segundo, California:TIP Publications (1986).

Hyde, J. S. "How Large Are Cognitive Gender Differences? A Meta-Analysis Using W2 and d," *American Psychologist,* 36:892–901 (1981).

Jenkins and Jenkins. Educational Leadership (Peer Tutoring) (1987).

Jenkins, Joseph R. and Linda M. Jenkins. "Making Peer Tutoring Work," *Educational Leadership,* 44(6) (March 1987).

Johnson, D. W., R. T. Johnson and E. J. Holubec. *Circles of Learning: Cooperation in the Classroom,* Edina, Minn:Intervention Book Co. (1986).

Johnson, Vernon. *I'll Quit Tomorrow,* San Francisco, CA:Harper and Row (1980).

Kellam, Sheppard. "Prevention Research on Early Risk Behaviors," conference paper, World Health Organization, 1986, in ASCD Update (February 1987).

Kenney, Anita M. and Margaret Orr, Terry. *Sex Education: An Overview of Current Programs, Policies and Research,* Bloomington, Ind.:Phi Delta Kappan, Vol. 65, No. 7, Maier (1984).

Kerman, S. and M. Martin. *Teacher Expectations and Student Achievement—TESA,* Bloomington, Indiana:Phi Delta Kappan (1980).

Lippett, P. *Students Teach Students,* Fastback No. 65, Phi Delta Kappan, Educational Foundation (1975).

Maker, Janice C. *Critical Issues in Gifted Education,* Rockville, Maryland:Aspen Publishers, Inc., 186.

Matriello, G. "Managing the Culture of the School," *Educational Leadership,* 42(2):80–86 (1986).

Mosston, Muska. *Teaching Physical Education,* Columbus, Ohio:Charles E. Merrill (1966).

Muraskin, Laura. "Sex Education Mandates: Are They The Answer?" *Family Planning Perspectives,* Vol. 18 No. 6. p. 171. New York City:Alan Guttmacher Institute (September/October, 1985).

National Center on Child Abuse and Neglect, "Everything You Always Wanted to Know About Child Abuse," Washington, D.C. (1984).

National Diffusion Network. *Educational Programs That Work,* Edition 12. Longmont, Colorado:Sopris West, Inc. (1986).

Ogden, Evelyn, William Fowler and Daniel Kunz. "A Study of Strategies to Increase Student Achievement in Low Achieving Schools," paper presented at the American Educational Research Association Conference (March, 1982).

Pennsylvania Deparatment of Education. *Student Assistance Program Training Manual,* Harrisburg, Pa. (1986).

Pennsylvania Department of Education. *Student Assistance Program Training Manual,* Harrisburg, Pa., revised (1986).

Perkins, Hugh. "Classroom Behavior and Underachievement," *American Educational Research Journal,* 2:1–11 (January, 1968).

Rest, Ray C. "Students Social Class and Teacher Expectations: The Self-Fulfilling Prophecy in Ghetto Education," *Harvard Educational Review,* 40:411–451 (August, 1970).

Roberts, Fitzmahon and Associates. "Here's Looking At You, 2000," Educational Services District, #121 Seattle, Washington (1986).

Rosenshine, B. and N. Furst. "Research on Teacher Performance Criteria," in *Research in Teacher Education: A Symposium,* edited by B. O. Smith, Englewood Cliffs, N.J.:Prentice-Hall, Inc. (1971).

Rosenthal, R., and L. Jacobson. *Pygmalion in the Classroom: Teacher Expectations and Pupil's Intellectual Development,* Holt, Rinehart and Winston (1968).

Rutter, Michael. *Changing Youth in a Changing Society,* Cambridge, Mass.:Harvard University Press (1985).

Sandt, Roseann and Susan Tenzer. *Reflections of Recovery,* Center for Personal Development, 3:3 (Sept., 1986).

Scriptographic Booklet, "About Anorexia Nervosa," South Deerfield, MA.:Channing L. Bete Co. (1985).

Silverman, L. K., *Gifted Education,* St. Louis:C. V. Mosky (1986).

Stallings, J. and P. H. Kraskowitz. "Follow-through Classroom Observation Education," Menlo Park, Ca.:Stanford Research Institute (1972–73).

Strother, D. B. "Practical Applications of Research: Mental Health Education," *Phi Delta Kappan,* 65(2):140–141 (1983).

Turkinoff, W., D. Berliner and R. Rest. Abstract from *Special Study: An Enthrographic Study of the Forty Classrooms of the Beginning Teacher Evaluation Study Known Sample,* San Francisco:for West Laboratory (1975).

United States Department of Education. *What Works: Schools Without Drugs,* Washington, D.C. (1986).

University of Michigan Institute for Social Research, survey reported by Blanca Gonzales in "Delusions of Grandeur," *School Safety* (Spring 1986).

Wayson, W. W. and T. J. Lasley. *Climate for Excellence: Schools that Foster Self Discipline,* Phi Delta Kappan, 65(6):419–421 (1984).

Weiner, Roberta. *AIDS: Impact on the Schools,* A Special Report from the Education Research Group, Arlington, Virginia (1986).

Weiner, Roberta (executive editor). *Teen Pregnancy: Impact on Schools,* a report from the Education Research Group, Alexandria, Virginia:Capitol Publications, Inc. (1987).

Zabin, Laurie, et al. "School-Based Clinics: A National Conference," *Family Planning Perspectives* (January/February, 1986).

Index

About the Authors

Evelyn Hunt Ogden

Dr. Ogden received her Ed.D. from Rutgers University in Educational and Psychological Measurement and Statistics. She is the author of major studies and reports on effective and ineffective schools, programs that work, strategies to increase student achievement, reduction of school violence and dissemination of successful practices in education. She currently serves on the US Department of Education panel which reviews the effectiveness of educational programs (JDRP). Her twenty years of administrative experience in education has included roles as Deputy Assistant Commissioner for Planning, New Jersey Department of Education; Director of Assistance to the National Diffusion Network (NDN); Director of Curriculum, Moorestown, New Jersey; and her current position as Deputy Superintendent, East Brunswick, New Jersey.

Vito Germinario

Dr. Germinario received his Ed.D. from Rutgers University in Educational Administration and Supervision. He has teaching experience at the junior high, high school and college level. He also taught at the Bordentown Youth Correctional Center for Men. Dr. Germinario has been an elementary and middle school principal and currently serves as Assistant Superintendent for the Moorestown Township Public Schools in New Jersey. Dr. Germinario has lectured and conducted workshops for numerous New Jersey school districts and private organizations on such topics as the supervision of instruction, essentials of instruction and verbal interaction in the classroom.

173